PASCAL
A CONSIDERATE APPROACH

DAVID PRICE

A SPECTRUM BOOK

Prentice-Hall, Inc., Englewood Cliffs, N.J. 07632

Library of Congress Cataloging in Publication Data

Price, David, 1910–
   Pascal : a considerate approach.

   "A Spectrum Book."
   Includes index.
   1. PASCAL (Computer program language)   I. Title.
QA76.73.P2P74   001.64'24   81-22664
                                           AACR2
   71284
ISBN 0-13-652818-X

ISBN 0-13-652800-7 {PBK.}

This Spectrum Book is available to businesses and organizations
at a special discount when ordered in large quantities. For
information, contact Prentice-Hall, Inc., General Publishing
Division, Special Sales, Englewood Cliffs, N.J. 07632.

10   9   8   7   6   5   4   3   2   1

Printed in the United States of America

Prentice-Hall International, Inc., London
Prentice-Hall of Australia Pty. Limited, Sidney
Prentice-Hall of Canada, Ltd., Toronto
Prentice-Hall of India Private Limited, New Delhi
Prentice-Hall of Japan, Inc., Tokyo
Prentice-Hall of Southeast Asia Pte. Ltd., Singapore
Whitehall Books Limited, Wellington, New Zealand

Contents

Preface

This book presents a complete introduction to the programming language Pascal. No prior programming experience is assumed. Neither is any advanced mathematical training.

Clear explanations are combined with sample programs to make new programming concepts easy to apply. At the same time, the idea of "considerate programming" is presented. The aim of considerate programming is to produce computer programs that are easy to read and easy to use. With the considerate approach, program development also becomes simpler and less perplexing.

1

What is Pascal?

Pascal is an easily mastered computer language. With a little practice, you will soon be able to express complex instructions in the form of Pascal programs. If you already know another computer language, like BASIC or FORTRAN, you will find Pascal to be quite different--and probably quite attractive.

Pascal was designed from the beginning to be used by people who aren't necessarily computer experts. It was created by Professor Niklaus Wirth at Eidgenossische Technische Hochschule in Zurich, Switzerland. Although it was originally conceived as a vehicle for teaching good programming techniques, it has since become popular outside academia as well.

A computer language is a medium of expression. Just as a human language (like English) is a medium for communication between two people, a computer language is a medium for communication between a person and a computer. Unlike English, however, computer languages do not allow for ambiguous meanings. Each computer language has a rigidly defined grammar known as its syntax. If a program statement is not syntactically correct, that statement is meaningless. Conversely, a syntactically correct statement can have only one meaning.

1

A computer program is simply a sequence of statements. The statements represent instructions for a computer to follow in performing the desired task. The method used by the program to perform its task is called its algorithm; it is up to the programmer to select the algorithm that his or her program will embody. An algorithm might be a simple mathematical equation, like the quadratic formula, or it might be a complicated procedure. In either case, it is the job of the programmer to express the algorithm in the form of a computer program.

Not unnaturally, different programmers have different ideas of how programs should be written. Some programmers strive to write programs with the smallest number of statements or with the fastest running time. The view of programming presented in this book measures program quality by another standard altogether. A good program, in this view, is one written so that other people can understand it. More specifically, this means that a programmer should

1.   write programs that are easy to read, and
2.   write programs that are easy to use.

Taken together, these aims are referred to in this book as considerate programming. If you have grown accustomed to the idea that computer programming is strictly a machine-oriented discipline, then this terminology may sound a bit out of place. Computer programming is not, however, as machine-oriented as you might think. Since computers exist for the purpose of serving people, computer programming is ultimately a "people-oriented" discipline as well. An important asset of a computer programmer, then, is his concern for the people who will read and use his programs. The aims outlined here may seem obvious, but in real life they aren't always so simple to achieve. The apparently straightforward task of writing a good program requires a deliberate, conscientious effort. When writing a program, one is often tempted to sacrifice clarity in exchange for some petty efficiency. Fortunately, Pascal is well suited for the type of programming that yields lucid programs. Its systematic design imposes a great deal of discipline, yet it also permits you to extend the language with new features that meet special needs. In short, Pascal makes it easier for a programmer to write good programs.

2
What does a Pascal program look like?

2.1   A VERY SIMPLE PROGRAM

Suppose you wanted to write a program that calculates the sum of two numbers. How would you do it? What would the completed program look like? To help you get acquainted with the characteristic style of Pascal, Example 2.1 shows the form that this program might take.

```
EXAMPLE 2.1:   The sum of two numbers

        program SUMS(INPUT,OUTPUT) ;
        var
            ADDEND1,ADDEND2,RESULT : INTEGER ;
        begin
            ADDEND1 := 3 ;
            ADDEND2 := 4 ;
            RESULT := ADDEND1+ADDEND2 ;
            WRITELN(RESULT)
        end.
```

Now, what does all this mean?

Let's start by dividing the program into smaller parts. The first line of the program is called the header. Its purpose is simply to specify the program name we have chosen. In this case, the program was named SUMS. If we had instead chosen the name ADDER, the header line would have looked like this:

program ADDER (INPUT,OUTPUT) ;

In Example 2.1, as in future examples, some words are printed entirely in lower case. These words are called reserved words, because they each have a special meaning in Pascal. The word program, for instance, tells us that we are reading the header line. Other reserved words mean different things. (Although it is unnecessary to make any typographic distinction as far as the computer is concerned, reserved words appear in lower case throughout this book to make the sample programs more readable for you.)

2.2   THE VARIABLE DECLARATIONS

After the header, the next two lines of the sample program comprise the variable declaration statement. This statement tells the computer how many variables we want to use in our program, what their names will be, and what type of data we want to store in them. In the program named SUMS, we have declared three variables, named ADDEND1, ADDEND2, and RESULT. All of them are of type INTEGER, which means that they can represent only integers.

What exactly is a variable? For our purposes, we can consider a variable to be a simple "black box" in which data can be stored. A variable of type INTEGER, for example, can store one integer number. In later chapters we will discuss other data types; until then, the example programs will use only integer variables.

There are few restrictions on the names we can give to variables. They can be sensible words, like RESULT, or nonsense words, like ZBLICN. As you can see, sensible names are much better, because they make the program easier to understand. In particular, we should always strive to select variable names that describe the

purpose of the variable. This way, we will not
become confused later about which variable corresponds to which task.

Here are the most important restrictions
on selection of variable names:

1.   Variable names cannot be reserved words.
     Thus we could not declare variables named
     PROGRAM or VAR. (Appendix 1 contains a more
     complete list of the reserved words.)
2.   Variable names must start with a letter.
     Thus, the name ADDEND1 is acceptable, but
     1ADDEND is not.
3.   Variable names can be any length, but some
     versions of Pascal pay attention to only the
     first eight characters. In that case, the
     names ACCOUNTSPAYABLE and ACCOUNTSRECEIVABLE
     would refer to the same variable.

After we have declared all the variables that
our program will use, we are ready to put them to
work. We can assign them values, use them in program calculations, and print them. This brings us
to the final section of the example program.

2.3   THE PROGRAM BODY

Here is where all the action happens. Everything
we have seen so far--the header and then the
declarations--has been getting the computer (and
us) ready for the body of the program. This is
the section that indicates the sequence of operations we want the computer to perform.

The program body is enclosed by two reserved
words: begin and end. These words function like
a pair of parentheses. When used to mark the
conclusion of a program, end is also followed by a
period. This punctuation is important because, as
we will find later, a begin ... end block can also
be used for other purposes. (To simplify things,
we will temporarily ignore the placement of the
semicolons, which are another important aspect of
Pascal punctuation.)

The first three lines of the body in the sample program are assignment statements. As you
might expect, the purpose of an assignment statement is to assign a value to some variable. The
value can be an arbitrary number, like 3 or 4, or
it can be a mathematical expression, like ADDEND1+

ADDEND2.   Other operations available for integer arithmetic include:

-	subtract
*	multiply
div	integer divide
mod	remainder from division
ABS	absolute value
SQR	square

No matter how complicated the expression, it will be calculated accurately by the computer using the standard algebraic precedence rules. (As in ordinary mathematical notation, parentheses can be used to override the precedence rules.)   Here are some examples of integer expressions in Pascal:

9-4	(equals 5)
6*7	(equals 42)
6+3*8	(equals 30)
(6+3)*8	(equals 72)
9 div 3	(equals 3)
10 div 3	(equals 3)
9 mod 3	(equals 0)
10 mod 3	(equals 1)
ABS(-5)	(equals 5)
SQR(4)	(equals 16)

If you ever have trouble remembering the order of operation precedence, just remember the phrase "My Dear Aunt Sally."   The abbreviation MDAS gives you the order in which terms are evaluated: multiplications and divisions first, then additions and subtractions.   Operations of equal precedence are evaluated left to right. Thus:

1+2*3 = 7	(not 9)
2+6 div 2 = 5	(not 4)

One of the operations, mod, may seem strange to you. Mod stands for modulo; its purpose is to find the remainder of an integer division operation.   The expression i mod j is equivalent to the expression

i - (i div j)*j

The mod operation is very handy. Since div returns only the integer part of the quotient, we can use <u>mod</u> to find the remainder. <u>Mod</u> also has other uses: for instance, if x mod 2 equals 0, then we know that x is even; if x mod 2 equals 1, then we know that x is odd.

What is the effect of an assignment? Simply this: the variable on the left of the <u>:=</u> sign is given the value of the expression on the right of the <u>:=</u> sign. In the sample program, ADDEND1 is set equal to 3, and ADDEND2 is set equal to 4. RESULT then takes the value of 7, because (ADDEND1 +ADDEND2)=(3+4)=7.

A variable that has been declared, but not yet given a value, is considered to be <u>undefined</u>. An undefined variable has no value. If we try to use an undefined variable in a program calculation, the program will not work. Example 2.2 below shows an ailing program that tries to use variable <u>ADDEND2</u> before it has been defined.

<u>EXAMPLE 2.2</u>: <u>A Program That Won't Work</u>

```
program NOGOOD(INPUT,OUTPUT) ;
var
    ADDEND1,ADDEND2,RESULT : INTEGER ;
begin
    ADDEND1 := 3 ;
    RESULT : ADDEND1 + ADDEND2 ;    ⊗
    ADDEND2 := 4 ;
    WRITELN(RESULT)
end.
```

The program will fail when it reaches this statement, because ADDEND2 does not have a value yet.

Some assignment statements look peculiar, even though they are perfectly acceptable to the computer. Here is a problem for you to solve: after covering the next paragraph with your hand, try to determine the effect of the assignment.

$$AGE := age + 1$$

As you may have guessed, this assignment increases the value of AGE by 1. Suppose AGE equals 5. When this assignment statement is encountered, the computer will evaluate the expression (AGE+1)=(5+1)=6. So the new value of AGE is 6. Similarly, <u>AGE:=AGE-1</u> would decrease AGE by 1. (Of course, if AGE had no prior value, these assignments would yield the "undefined value" error that we just discussed.)

When a variable is given a new value, what happens to the old value? It is simply erased. Since a variable of type INTEGER can store only one number, each successive assignment to that variable destroys its preceding values. A variable always contains the result of its most recent assignment.

In Example 2.1, only one statement is left. WRITELN, while not a reserved word, is a Pascal verb that has a special meaning. The WRITELN statement instructs the computer to display specific data on the user's input-output terminal, which might be a teletypewriter or a video display console. The items to be displayed are listed inside a pair of parentheses. An item within the list can be a number, a variable, a mathematical expression, or even ordinary words. Here are some valid WRITELN statements:

```
WRITELN(52,52*2,52*3)
WRITELN(RESULT*2)
WRITELN(ABS(DEFICIT))
WRITELN(DIVISOR div DIVIDEND)
WRITELN('This sentence will be printed
        verbatim.')
```

Assuming that RESULT, DEFICIT, DIVISOR, and DIVIDEND have been declared and have a value, these WRITELN statements will print the results of the expressions(s) listed. The final example in the series demonstrates the use of character strings in WRITELN statements. The characters inside the single quotation marks will be printed as they stand. We can even mix character strings and expressions within a single WRITELN, like this:

```
WRITELN('The area of the given rectancle is ',
        LENGTH*WIDTH)
```

Chapter three will discuss the WRITELN statement and other input-output statements in greater detail. Before moving on to that, let's take a quick look at the care and feeding of semicolons.

2.4   WHAT ARE THE SEMICOLONS FOR?

Semicolons are used in Pascal to separate statements. In general, every statement should be terminated by a semicolon. There are only a few exceptions to this rule. You have encountered the most frequently used of these exceptions already: the begin...end construct.

The reserved word begin is never followed by a semicolon, and the reserved word end is never preceded by one. To see why the begin...end construct is a special case, consider the structure of a begin...end block:

$$\text{begin } S_1;\ S_2;\ S_3;\ \dots\ S_{n-1};\ S_n \text{ end}$$

Remember that begin and end are like parentheses. In this diagram, each S represents a single statement. You would not add extra semicolons to the notation

$$(S_1;\ S_2;\ S_3;\ S_4)$$

Likewise, you should not put a semicolon after a begin or before an end in Pascal. Notice that these guidelines are borne out in Example 2.1. To become more familiar with semicolon use, just keep your good eye open when you read the sample programs.

2.5 SYNTAX ERRORS

Just as English has a formal grammar of sorts, computer languages have rigid grammars--or syntaxes--all their own. Needless to say, a programmer using Pascal (or any other language) must be careful to observe the rules of correct syntax. Common syntax errors include misuse of semicolons, misspelling of reserved words, and other trifling details. Novice programmers are usually quick to ask, "Why can't the computer correct my syntax errors for me?"

A more experienced programmer would reply, "For the computer to fix your errors, it must first know what you meant to say." In other words, computers can't read minds, as yet. Diagnosing and correcting errors is not a mechanical process. As you will discover, this process is often the most challenging phase of program development. There is even a special slang for it: the process of diagnosing and correcting errors is called debugging; it covers not only syntax errors, but also the errors that become apparent during program execution. The errors in a program are consequently referred to as <u>bugs</u>.

THE ASSIGNMENT OPERATOR

Symbol: :=

General form: <u>variable</u> := <u>expression</u>

The assignment operator sets <u>variable</u> equal to the value obtained when <u>expression</u> is evaluated. Both items, <u>variable</u> and <u>expression</u>, should be of the same type. For instance, if the variable specified is of type INTEGER, then the expression should yield an integer value.

Examples:

    COUNT := COUNT+1

    PAY := WAGE*HOURS

    FORCE := MASS*ACCEL

    RETAILPRICE := WHOLESALEPRICE*2

In this book, major components of Pascal syntax will be defined inside boxes like the one above. These definitions are placed outside the text itself so they will be easier to find and use for reference.

<u>Problem Set</u>

*1.   Write a program that calculates the area of a triangle whose base is 3 centimeters and whose height is 5 centimeters. The output of your program should be comprehensible to someone who is unfamiliar with the program. Be sure to use variable names that reflect the purpose of the variable.

 2.   Suppose that Pascal variable names could be only one character long. That is, variables like R and V would be permitted, but RATE and VELOCITY would not. What undesirable effects would this restriction have?

*This asterisk indicates that the solutions to these questions may be found in Appendix 5 at the end of the book.

*3.   Using integer expressions, write assignment
      statements that are equivalent to these
      formulas:

      $A = LW$

      $M = R^3/P^2$

      $S = \dfrac{Y_1 - Y_2}{X_1 - X2}$

      $X = |A|$

4.   Correct the errors in this program.

```
program BUGLADEN(INPUT,OUTPUT)
var
      BEGIN : INTEGER ;
begin ;
      TEMP := 13 ;
      BEGIN := SQR(TEMP) ;
      WRITELN('Thirteen squared equals ',BEGIN
end.
```

3

Reading and printing information

3.1   WRITE AND WRITELN

We have already seen WRITELN in use. Now we are
going to discuss WRITELN, and its companion statement, WRITE, in a little more detail. A summary
of the two is shown in the accompanying box.

WRITE and WRITELN

General forms: WRITE(expression list)
                    WRITELN(expression list)

These statements are used to direct output to the user's
input-output terminal.

Examples:
    WRITE(' This is an example of a character string.')
    WRITELN(' Your tax bill for the year is $',TAX:5)
    WRITELN(ACRES:4,' acres remain unharvested.')

What is the difference between WRITE and
WRITELN?   They are exactly the same, with one

exception.   Let's look at the effects of a pair
of WRITELN statements.

```
WRITELN('This is the first line.  ')
WRITELN('This is the second.')
```

As you know, this sequence of statements will
produce the following output:

```
This is the first line.
This is the second.
```

After the first WRITELN was executed, the
output that followed started on a new line. This
is because the WRITELN statement, after printing
its   expression   list,   automatically   moves   the
printhead or cursor of the user's terminal to the
beginning of the next line.   If the two statements in the example had been WRITEs instead of
WRITELNs, here is what would have been printed:

```
This is the first line.  This is the second.
```

The output from both statements was printed
on the same line.   The WRITE statement, then,
does not advance the print position after completion.   Except for a few cases, you will generally
use WRITELN.   (You might use WRITE if you had an
unwieldy expression list that you wanted to fit
on one output line, for example.)
When you are printing integer values, you may
want to specify the desired field length for each
value.   The field length of a value is the number
of print positions allocated to that value.   When
the field length is not specified, most versions
of Pascal use a default field length of 12.   In
that case, the statement

```
WRITELN(' The deficit is ',DEBTS)
```

would produce this output, where DEBTS equals 1500:

```
The deficit is        1500
```

That looks peculiar, doesn't it?   The eight
extra spaces are there to pad the twelve-column
field.   Whenever a value is smaller than its output field, Pascal adds extra blanks on the left
to make up the difference.   Fortunately, there is
a way to specify smaller field lengths.   If we

wanted DEBTS to have a field length of four columns, we would say:

WRITELN(' The deficit is ',DEBTS:4)

The number following the colon indicates the desired field length. In this statement, DEBTS is allocated four columns. If DEBTS were larger than that (i.e., if it were greater than 9999), its value would automatically be printed in a larger field. Example 3.1 shows a program that specifies a minimum field width for all the integer values output.

EXAMPLE 3.1: The Average Of Three Numbers

```
program AVERAGE(INPUT,OUTPUT) ;
var
     FIRST,SECOND,THIRD : INTEGER ;
     SUM : INTEGER ;
begin
     FIRST := 5;
     SECOND := 17 ;
     THIRD := 8 ;
     SUM := FIRST+SECOND+THIRD ;
     WRITELN(' The average of ',FIRST:4,', ',SECOND:4,
             ' and') ;
     WRITELN(THIRD:4,' is ',(SUM div 3):3)
end.
```

It is also possible to print a blank line. We might do this to separate groups of related data. Some versions of Pascal let you program a blank line with a very simple statement:

WRITELN

Other versions make you go to a little more trouble:

WRITELN(' ')

3.2 THE READ STATEMENT

Consider the program shown in Example 3.1. Its purpose is to find the average of three numbers. As the program stands, it calculates the average of 5, 17, and 8. If we wanted to use this program to find the average of another set of numbers, we would have to rewrite several assignment statements.

Who wants to do all that work? The whole point of using a computer is to save work, not to create it. We ought to be able to write a program once, and then use the program many times under different circumstances. When we use AVERAGE, we should be able to specify the numbers we want averaged without having to monkey with the program statements. Pascal provides a statement that allows us this kind of flexibility. The statement is called READ, and it is summarized in the accompanying box. (The READLN statement will be discussed in section 3.3.)

READ and READLN

General forms: READ(variable,variable...)
                     READLN(variable,variable ...)

These statements are used to obtain input data from the user's input-output terminal.

Examples:
    READ(HOURS)
    READ(DAY,MONTH,YEAR)
    READLN(RADIUS)
    READLN(GROSSPAY,NETPAY)

Now we can modify AVERAGE so that it will accept a new set of values each time it is run. Example 3.2 shows how the new AVERAGE program might look. In the new program, FIRST, SECOND, and THIRD do not take their values from assignment statements. Instead, their values are entered directly from the user's terminal.

Example 3.2:   An Interactive Averaging Program

```
program AVERAGE2(INPUT,OUTPUT) ;
var
      FIRST,SECOND,THIRD : INTEGER ;
      SUM : INTEGER ;
begin
      WRITELN(' Please enter the three numbers you
      want averaged:') ;
      READ(FIRST,SECOND,THIRD) ;
      SUM := FIRST+SECOND+THIRD ;
      WRITELN(' The  average  of ',FIRST:4,',  ',SECOND:4,
             ' and') ;
      WRITELN(THIRD:4,' is ',(SUM div 3):3)
end.
```

The new program, AVERAGE2, is certainly more useful than the old one. When the READ statement is encountered, the computer will stop and wait for input. After the three numbers are entered, each of the variables listed after the READ will take on the value of one of the numbers. FIRST will take the value of the first number entered, and so on. Here is a demonstration of AVERAGE2 in action:

```
Please enter the three numbers you want
averaged:
3     52     -27

The average of     3,    52 and
 -27 is    9
```

3.3   THE READLN STATEMENT

READLN is a variant of the READ statement. The relationship between READ and READLN is analogous to that between WRITE and WRITELN. READLN accepts data one line at a time, while READ accepts data as a continuous "stream."

Inside the computer, each line of input data is terminated with an end-of-line marker. The READ statement ignores this marker, but the READLN statement uses it to determine which data it will fetch. After reading all the variables listed inside the parentheses, READLN discards the rest of that line. For instance, suppose the following input line is entered:

    7   15   3   48

The statement READLN(X,Y) would set X equal
to 7 and Y equal to 15. All further input on
that line would then be discarded. The statement
READ(X,Y), however, would leave 3 and 48 available
for later use.

3.4 DESIGN YOUR OUTPUT

The design of program output is an important
aspect of considerate programming. It is one
thing to write a program that works; it is
another thing to write a program with well
designed output. You can start off on the right
foot by keeping one basic idea in mind: the
person who uses your program is not omniscient.

That is certainly a reasonable proposition,
isn't it? The people who use your program will
have no idea what goes on inside it--nor should
they. Consequently, it is unreasonable to expect
them to decipher incoherent output. It is also
unreasonable to expect them to understand obscure
abbreviations or to interpret vague instructions.

EXAMPLE 3.3: A Program With Undesirable Output

```
program AVOID(INPUT,OUTPUT) ;
var
     FIRST,SECOND,THIRD : INTEGER ;
     SUM : INTEGER ;
begin
     WRITELN(' What numbers?') ;
     READ(FIRST,SECOND,THIRD) ;
     SUM  := FIRST+SECOND+THIRD ;
     WRITELN(SUM div 3)
end.
```

Example 3.3 is a program that makes unreasonable expectations of its users. Compare the
prompting phrase ("What numbers?") with that of
Example 3.2. Upon reading the new phrase, an
unfamiliar user would probably wonder, "How many

numbers am I supposed to enter?" He might even wonder, "What are the numbers going to be used for?"

The report of the results is unsatisfactory, too. When the calculations are completed, this program prints only a number, with no explanation. What good is an isolated number, unless we have been told what it represents? Novelists can leave things up to their readers' imaginations, but considerate programmers do not allow themselves similar license.

Problem Set

*1. What output will the following statement sequence produce?

```
WRITELN(' It is important') ;
WRITE('not to ') ;
WRITELN('confuse WRITE') ;
WRITELN(' ') ;
WRITE('with WRITELN.') ;
WRITELN('Their effects are') ;
WRITE('quite different.') ;
```

 2. Write a program that will read three integers representing a month, a day, and a year. The program should then print this date in the conventional mm-dd-yy format. For instance, the input

        9   3   1961

should yield the output

        9-3-61

*3. Convert the program shown in Example 2.1 so that it can be used with different sets of addends. Be sure to design readable output.

 4. A hypothetical stock portfolio is presently valued at $10,000, evenly divided among five stocks. Write a program to calculate the future value of the portfolio. After the user enters his or her predictions of the percentage change in the price of each stock, the program should report what the new value of the portfolio would be.

4

More
built-in data types

4.1 THE DATA TYPE REAL

All our programs so far have used only variables of type INTEGER. Thus, we have been restricted to performing integer arithmetic. Most computer applications, however, require some form of non-integer arithmetic. In fact, any application that involves fractional quantities also involves, by definition, real numbers. To keep track of dollar amounts, a simple bookkeeping program will require real numbers. Scientific computations, especially those incorporating logarithmic or trigonometric functions, will also require real numbers.

Fortunately, Pascal provides a built-in data type called REAL. We can declare variables to be of type REAL the same way we declare integer variables. We can also incorporate real arithmetic into mathematical expressions. The operators permitted in real arithmetic are the same as those allowed in integer arithmetic, except for the division symbol. In real arithmetic, the reserved word <u>div</u> is replaced by the symbol /. Unlike integer division, which yields only the integer part of the quotient, real division returns the entire result. Thus:

           5 div 2 = 2
     but   5/2 = 2.5

A number of predefined functions are also available. The functions mentioned in Chapter 2, ABS(x) and SQR(x), can be used with reals. In addition, the following functions accept either a real or an integer argument and return a real result:

SIN(x)	sine of x in radians
COS(x)	cosine of x in radians
EXP(x)	e^x
LN(x)	natural logarithm of x (with x>0)
SQRT(x)	square root of x (with x≥0)
ARCTAN(x)	arctangent of x in radians

These functions can be used within any arithmetic expression. Their arguments can, in turn, be expressions themselves. This means that real expressions, like integer expressions, can be as complex as you need to make them.

EXAMPLE 4.1:   Computing Sines And Cosines


```
program TRIG(INPUT,OUTPUT) ;
var
     ANGLE : REAL ;
     RESULT1,RESULT2 : REAL ;
begin
     WRITELN(' What is the radian measure of the
     angle?') ;
     READ(ANGLE) ;
     RESULT1 := SIN(ANGLE) ;
     RESULT2 := COS(ANGLE) ;
     WRITELN(' The sine is ',RESULT1:6:3) ;
     WRITELN(' The cosine is ',RESULT2:6:3)
end.
```

The program shown in Example 4.1 declares three variables: ANGLE, RESULT1, and RESULT2. The final WRITELN statements demonstrate how to specify a field width for a real number. The field width specification for a real number should be in the form :w:d, where w indicates the total field width

and d indicates the number of digits to the right
of the decimal point. If the sample program were
given an angle of 1.047 radians--that is, $\pi/3$--the
output would look like this:

        The sine is   0.866
        The cosine is   0.500

    If we hadn't specified d, or if we hadn't
specified any field width at all, the output would
have been printed in scientific notation:

        The sine is 8.65927E-01
        The cosine is 5.00000E-01

    In this form of scientific notation, the E
means "times ten to the power of." The number to
the right of the E is the exponent part. (Remember that the capital E used here is not the same
as the mathematical symbol e.) Scientific notation is not as unnatural as it may seem. As long
as you remember what the E stands for, you won't
have any problems. For example:

        $5.00000\text{E-}01 = 5*10^{-1} = 0.5$
        $5.00000\text{E+}00 = 5*10^{0} = 5.0$
        $5.00000\text{E+}01 = 5*10^{1} = 50.0$

        $6.37104\text{E+}03 = 6.37104*10^{3} = 6371.04$

        $7.0\text{E-}02 = 7.0*10^{-2} = 0.007$

    Scientific notation is convenient when you
need to write a number that is very large or very
small. The conversion factor called Avogadro's
Number, frequently encountered in freshman chem-
istry classes, might be found in an assignment
statement like this:

        ATOMS := MOLES * 6.02E+23

    In most versions of Pascal, real numbers can
retain up to six significant digits of accuracy.
The number 1.234567, for instance, will usually be
rounded   to   1.23457.   Likewise,   the   number
7.654321E+10 will be rounded to 7.65432E+10. This
discrepancy may seem tiny, but in some programs
even a small degree of error can accumulate into
an undesirable one.
    The inaccuracies that arise from rounding
can sometimes lead to bizarre results. Although
they do not affect every program, it pays to keep

an eye open for them. You cannot, for instance,
always rely on the simple equality "X = 3*(X/3)".
Why? Here is how the expression works out for two
values of X:

        for X=3.0, 3*(X/3) = 3*1.00000 = 3.0
   but for X=1.0, 3*(X/3) = 3*0.33333 = 0.99999

     Fortunately, this error isn't as serious as
it looks.   An output statement with a suitable
field width will cause the inaccurate value to
be rounded automaticaly when it is printed.   For
example, with X equal to 0.99999, the statement
WRITELN(X:4:2) would actually print 1.00.
     Some versions of Pascal provide more than
six digits of accuracy in real numbers.   When
you write programs using the type REAL, you
should be aware of the precision available from
your particular machine.   You should also remember that transcendental functions, such as SIN
and LN, usually generate results with fewer digits
of precision than the other operations.

4.2   INTERACTION OF INTEGERS AND REALS

     If a real variable is assigned an integer value,
the integer value is automatically converted into
its real equivalent.   An integer variable, however,
cannot be assigned a real value. Thus, if COUNT is
an integer variable, the following assignments will
cause a type mismatch error:

        COUNT := 3.14
        COUNT := SQRT(2)
        COUNT := 0.5

     An integer variable obviously cannot take a
value like 0.5, because 0.5 has no integer representation.   That is why these assignments will
cause a program to fail.   (Of course, if COUNT
were declared to be of type REAL, these assignments would be perfectly acceptable.)
     To get around this limitation, we can use
Pascal's type transfer functions. These functions
accept a real value as an argument and convert it
into an integer value:

        TRUNC(x)   returns the integer part of x
        ROUND(x)   returns x rounded to the
                        nearest integer

Are these functions different? In some cases they both return the same value. For x = 3.2, TRUNC and ROUND both return 3. But for x = 3.6, TRUNC still returns 3, while ROUND returns 4. This happens because ROUND looks at the fractional part to decide whether to round x up or down, while TRUNC discards the fractional part altogether. Thus,

```
TRUNC(5.8)     →   5
ROUND(5.8)     →   6
TRUNC(3.14)    →   3
ROUND(3.14)    →   3
TRUNC(-7.7)    →   -7
ROUND(-7.7)    →   -8
```

If any term of an expression is of type REAL, then the entire expression returns a real result. Remember that the real functions listed in section 4.1, such as SQRT, _always_ return a real result. This means that SQRT(4) technically has the real value 2.0, not the integer value 2. Before it could be assigned to an integer variable, it would have to be converted into an integer value by one of the type transfer functions.

4.3   THE DATA TYPE BOOLEAN

Variables do not always have to represent numbers. One non-numeric type in Pascal is the data type BOOLEAN. A boolean variable can have either of two values: _true_ or _false_. Compared with the type REAL, which allows millions of discrete values, the type BOOLEAN may not appear very helpful. Strangely enough, though, it is the limited range of boolean values that gives boolean expressions their power.

Boolean expressions can take several forms. First, they can be the simple constants _true_ or _false_. Assignments using this form are analogous to numerical assignments like "ADDEND1 := 3." Here are two statements that assign boolean values to boolean variables:

```
FLAG := TRUE
VALID := FALSE
```

```
COMPARISONS

   =    equals
   >    greater than
   >=   greater than or equal
   <    less than
   <=   less than or equal
   <>   not equal
```

Boolean expressions can also be used to test comparisons. Suppose that we have two variables of type INTEGER and that we want to know whether they are unequal. If the variables are named FIRST and SECOND, we would test for their equality with the boolean expression

FIRST = SECOND

If the two are equal, this expression will have the value TRUE. If they are not equal, the expression will have the value FALSE. Notice that the equals sign (=) is different from the assignment symbol (:=). The other comparison symbols are listed in the accompanying box.
In addition, boolean expressions can be constructed from boolean operators. These operators are the fundamental tools of boolean logic, an algebra of logic devised by nineteenth-century mathematician George Boole. Pascal provides three boolean operators: and, or, and not. The first, and, is true only if both of its operands are true. Otherwise, it yields the value FALSE. Thus.

```
    TRUE and TRUE    →    TRUE
   FALSE and FALSE   →    FALSE
    TRUE and FALSE   →    FALSE
   FALSE and TRUE    →    FALSE
```

The second operator, or, is true if either of its operands are true. In other words, it is false only when both of its operands are false. Thus,

```
    TRUE or TRUE    →    TRUE
   FALSE or FALSE   →    FALSE
    TRUE or FALSE   →    TRUE
   FALSE or TRUE    →    TRUE
```

The third operator, not, takes one operand and returns its logical negation. That is, it returns

FALSE if the operand is true, and TRUE if the operand is false. Thus,

        not TRUE   →   FALSE
        not FALSE →   TRUE

What good do these operators do us? When we want to test for multiple conditions, they turn out to be very helpful. Suppose we have four real variables: HOURS1, HOURS2, WAGES1, and WAGES2. We will test for various conditions and place the results of the tests in boolean variable DUMMY. If we wanted to determine whether HOURS1 equals HOURS2, for example, we would simply write

        DUMMY := (HOURS1=HOURS2)

DUMMY now contains the boolean results of the comparison. If we wanted to know not only whether HOURS1 equals HOURS2, but also whether WAGES1 equals WAGES2, we would use the and operator:

        DUMMY := (HOURS1=HOURS2) and (WAGES1=WAGES2)

If both comparisons are true, then the and conjunction is true. If either comparison proves false, then the and conjunction is false. A similar test could be constructed to determine whether either equality is true:

        DUMMY := (HOURS1=HOURS2) or (WAGES1=WAGES2)

Later in the program, we could assign DUMMY the value of its logical negation:

        DUMMY := not DUMMY

As with integer and real expressions, boolean expressions can be as complex as you like. They can use the three boolean operators in any combination; operands can be simple boolean constants, boolean variables, or comparisons. As long as you use parentheses to indicate your intentions, you do not have to learn the precedence order for boolean expressions. The precedence order is listed in the box, however, for your reference.

```
┌─────────────────────────────────────────────────┐
│                                                   │
│  PRECEDENCE IN BOOLEAN EXPRESSIONS                │
│                                                   │
│                                                   │
│  highest    ( )                                   │
│             not                                   │
│             and                                   │
│             or                                    │
│  lowest     > =  < >  =  < =                       │
│                                                   │
│  Examples:                                        │
│             I and J or K   →   (I and J) or K     │
│             not X and Y    →   (not X) and Y      │
│                                                   │
└─────────────────────────────────────────────────┘
```

Pascal provides a predefined function, ODD(x), which takes an integer argument and returns a boolean value. If the integer expression x is odd, then ODD(x) is true; if x is even, then ODD(x) is false. We could create an equivalent test using the mod operator. For instance, the assignment

DUMMY := ODD(COUNT)

is equivalent to

DUMMY := (COUNT mod 2)=1

4.4 DECLARING CONSTANTS

In some programs, certain values are used in many different calculations. In a program involving trigonometry, for example, the real value 3.14159 would probably occur often. When this happens, it is convenient to give the value a name--to declare it as a constant. The program in Example 4.2 does just that. In a constant declaration, the identifier name on the left of the equals sign is symbolically "attached" to the constant on the right of the equals sign. In the rest of the program, the identifier is treated as if it were the original constant. The value on the right of the equals sign must be a simple constant; it cannot be an expression. Moreover, a constant cannot be assigned a new value after it has been declared. The constant declaration section always comes before the variable declarations. Unlike a variable declaration, constant declarations do not specify the data type used; the computer can

EXAMPLE 4.2:   Area and circumference of a circle

```
program CIRCLE(INPUT,OUTPUT) ;
const
    PI = 3.14159 ;
var
    RADIUS : REAL ;
begin
    WRITELN(' What is the radius of the circle? ')
    READ(RADIUS) ;
    WRITELN(' The circumference is ',(2*PI*RADIUS):6:2) ;
    WRITELN(' The area is ',(PI*SQR(RADIUS)):6:2)
end.
```

determine it by inspection. As you might guess, the rules for selecting constant identifiers are the same as those for selecting variable identifiers. Here are some valid constant declarations:

```
FREEZINGPOINT = 0
SPEEDLIMIT = 55
DAYSPERYEAR = 365.25
SPEEDOFLIGHT = 2.998E+10
DEVICEWORKING = TRUE
```

When you declare a constant and give it a meaningful name, you are adopting a more considerate stance towards the people who will meet your program later. First, symbolic constants make a program listing easier to understand. When others read your program for the first time, they will be grateful if you used identifiers (like WEEKSPERYEAR) instead of repetitively using unexplained values (like 52). The people reading your program may be able to figure out what the value represents, but time and mental energy will be conserved if you spell out your intentions by declaring the constant. (Even if you are the only one who will ever see the program, you should still apply good programming practices. Carelessly written programs can confound even their own authors.)

Second, symbolic constants make a program easier to modify. If we want to alter a value that occurs in expressions throughout the program, it is much simpler to change one line--a constant declaration--than to go through the program and change every occurrence of the value. For example, suppose you wanted to write a program that performs some calculation and then plots a series of points on the input-output terminal. To scale the points properly, the program would have to know the number of print positions available per line. Yet different terminals have different line lengths: some permit as many as 132 characters per line, while others permit only 80 or 72.

One way to write the program would be simply to write the line length into every expression that uses it. But if you later get a new terminal, or if you give the program to a friend who has a different terminal, then every reference to that value would have to be updated accordingly. A better approach would be to declare a constant:

    LINELENGTH = 80

Now you will be able to change the desired value by rewriting just one line. In one step, you have made the program both easier to read and easier to maintain. You can use LINELENGTH in an expression, as if it were a variable:

    SCALE := MAXVALUE/LINELENGTH

You can use it in a field width specification:

    WRITELN(TOTAL:LINELENGTH)

These statements will have the same effect as if the word LINELENGTH were directly replaced with the value 80. If you later changed the program so that LINELENGTH was set to 72, LINELENGTH would then be equated with 72 in the same way.

Pascal provides a predefined constant called MAXINT. The value of MAXINT varies from computer to computer; its value indicates the maximum integer that the computer can represent internally. If MAXINT equals 32,767 on your computer, then all integers must lie in the range -32,767 to +32,767. Assigning an integer variable a value outside this range would result in an overflow error. MAXINT usually equals 32,767 (or

$2^{15}-1$) on small computers and 2,147,483,647 (or

$2^{31}-1$) on large computers.

Problem Set

*1. Variables I and J have been declared INTEGER;
     variables X and Y have been declared REAL.
     Which of the following assignments would
     cause a type mismatch?

     X := SQRT(Y)
     X := SQRT(I)
     Y := SIN(J)
     I := SIN(X)
     J := COS(I)
     X := TRUNC(Y)
     J := X/I
     I := J * ROUND(X)

*2. If SUBTOTAL equals 17.693, what output would
     the following statements produce?

     WRITELN(SUBTOTAL:7:3)
     WRITELN(SUBTOTAL:7:2)
     WRITELN(SUBTOTAL:7:1)
     WRITELN(SUBTOTAL:5:1)
     WRITELN(SUBTOTAL:10)
     WRITELN(SUBTOTAL)

*3. We are given four boolean variables that
     contain information about a person. MARRIED
     is true if the person is married; BLOND is
     true if the person has blond hair; MALE is
     true if the person is a male; and EMPLOYED
     is true if the person has a job. Write
     boolean expressions to determine whether
     the person is

     -- a married woman
     -- a bachelor
     -- an unmarried blond
     -- an unemployed bachelorette
     -- either unmarried or unemployed or both

4.   Write a program that accepts two real numbers
     from the user. The program should then print
     the first number raised to the power of the
     second number. To perform exponentiation
     with real numbers in Pascal, use the follow-
     ing identity:

     $x^y = e^{y \ln x}$

5
Conditional statements

5.1 BRANCHING

Using boolean expressions, we can perform sophisticated tests on program conditions. We can test
to determine the boolean result of a comparison,
for example. Pascal provides a conditional statement, if...then...else, that lets us use the result
of a boolean expression to modify the flow of the
program.

IF...THEN...ELSE

General forms: if boolean then statement

                   if boolean then
                       statement$_1$
                   else
                       statement$_2$

In the first form, statement will be executed only if boolean
is true. In the second form, statement$_1$ will be executed if
boolean is true; if boolean is false, then statement$_2$ will be
executed instead.

Examples:

    if TEMP>O then FREEZING := FALSE

    if MARRIED then
       WRITELN(' The subject is married.')

    if I = J then
       WRITELN(' The numbers are equal.')
    else
       WRITELN(' The numbers are not equal.')

       The condition tested can be any boolean expression. This statement is called a <u>branching</u> statement because it allows the program flow to branch, depending on the result of the condition. After the action indicated by the <u>if</u> statement is executed, program flow continues starting at the next statement.

EXAMPLE 5.1:   Roots of quadratic equations

```
program QUADRATIC(INPUT,OUTPUT) ;
var
      QUAD,LINEAR,CON : INTEGER ;
      TEMP : INTEGER ;
begin
      WRITELN(' Please enter the coefficients of the') ;
      WRITELN(' quadratic, linear, and constant terms:') ;
      READ(QUAD,LINEAR,CON) ;
      TEMP := SQR(LINEAR) - 4*QUAD*CON ;
      if TEMP<O then
          WRITELN(' This equation has no real roots.') ;
      if TEMP = O then
          WRITELN(' This equation has one real root.') ;
      if TEMP>O then
          WRITELN(' This equation has two real roots.')
   end.
```

       The program in Example 5.1 accepts an equation in the form $Ax^2+Bx+C = O$, with A, B, and C represented by QUAD, LINEAR, and CON, respectively. The program then determines the number of real solutions for the equation. Since the conditions TEMP<O, TEMP=O, and TEMP>O are mutually exclusive, we could rewrite the program this way:

```
if TEMP<O then
    WRITELN(' This equation has no real roots.')
else
    if TEMP=O then
        WRITELN(' This equation has one
        real root.')
    else
        WRITELN(' This equation has two
        real root.')
```

When an _if_ statement occurs inside another _if_, the two are considered to be _nested_. In this program, nested _ifs_ are used to reduce the number of tests that must be made. This approach is often more efficient and concise, but it can also reduce program readability. As a rule of thumb, try not to nest an _if_ statement more than one or two levels. Beyond the second level of nesting, it becomes difficult to keep track of the conditions that each _if_ is testing.

When _else_ clauses are used with nested _ifs_, each _else_ corresponds to the _if_ immediately preceding it. Thus, there is no ambiguity in the preceding fragment. The first WRITELN is executed if TEMP<O, the second is executed if TEMP=O, and the third is executed if TEMP>O.

5.2   COMPOUND STATEMENTS

The _if_ control structure may seem inflexible, because the conditional action can be only one statement long. Sometimes we will want our programs to execute a _sequence_ of statements instead. In those cases, we would like to put an imaginary bracket around the sequence, like this:

```
if AMOUNTDUE > CREDITLIMIT then
   { WRITELN(' This customer has exceeded
   { the credit limit.')
   { ACCEPTORDER := FALSE
```

When we want to make a sequence of statements

act like a single statement, we can enclose the sequence inside the reserved words begin and end. The preceding if statement could be rewritten this way:

```
if AMOUNTDUE > CREDITLIMIT then
      begin
          WRITELN(' This customer has exceeded
                      the credit limit.') ;
          ACCEPTORDER := FALSE
      end ;
```

The begin...end block that we have formed here is called a compound statement. Compound statements are often used inside conditional statements (like if) so that the conditional action can be more than one statement long. The program shown in Example 5.2 uses a compound statement inside a nested if.

EXAMPLE 5.2:   The quadratic formula

```
program QUADFORMULA(INPUT,OUTPUT) ;
var
      QUAD,LINEAR,CON : REAL ;
      RADICAL,ROOT1,ROOT2 : REAL ;
begin
      WRITELN(' Please enter the coefficients of the') ;
      WRITELN(' quadratic, linear, and constant terms:') ;
      READ(QUAD,LINEAR,CON) ;
      RADICAL := SQR(LINEAR) - 4*QUAD*CON ;
      if RADICAL < O then
        WRITELN(' This equation has no real roots.')
      else
        if RADICAL = O then
          WRITELN(' This equation has the root ',
          -LINEAR/(2*QUAD))
        else
          begin
            ROOT1 := (-LINEAR+SQRT(RADICAL))/(2*QUAD) ;
            ROOT2 := (-LINEAR-SQRT(RADICAL))/(2*QUAD) ;
            WRITELN(' This equation has two roots: ',ROOT1) ;
            WRITELN(' and ',ROOT2)
          end
end.
```

Notice that not every statement in this example is terminated with a semicolon. Although
most statements in a Pascal program end with a
semicolon, some of them do not. We have already
mentioned one exception in Chapter 2: the reserved words begin and end. The rules governing semicolon usage are somewhat arbitrary, but at least
they are consistent. Here are three guidelines to
remember when writing Pascal programs:

1.   Each entry in the variable and constant
     declaration sections is terminated with a
     semicolon.
2.   Each statement in the program body is termin-
     ated with a semicolon, unless it is followed
     by the reserved words end, else, or until.
3.   Certain reserved words, such as then, else,
     var, const, and begin, are never terminated
     with a semicolon.

5.3   LOOPING

A loop is a statement sequence that can be
executed more than once. Pascal provides several
looping mechanisms, of which the simplest is the
while statement. When a while statement is
encountered, the specified action is executed
repetitively as long as the specified boolean
condition is true.

```
WHILE...DO


General form:        while boolean do
                         statement

The statement (or compound statement) specified will be
executed repetitively as long as boolean is true. If
boolean is false when the while is first encountered, then
the statement will not be executed.

Examples:
    while DEGREES > 180 do
       DEGREES := DEGREES - 360

    while COUNT < 10 do
       begin
          READ(NUMBER) ;
          SUN := SUM + NUMBER ;
          COUNT := COUNT + 1
       end
```

The program shown in Example 5.3 finds the average of a list of numbers; the size of the list is a symbolic constant. Each time a number is read, COUNT is incremented. Thus, the while loop will be executed exactly the number of times specified by LISTSIZE. For the program to work, both SUM and COUNT must be given initial values of zero before the while loop is entered.

EXAMPLE 5.3:   Averaging a list of arbitrary size

```
program AVERAGE3(INPUT,OUTPUT) ;
const
    LISTSIZE = 10 ;
var
    SUM,NUMBER : REAL ;
    COUNT : INTEGER ;
begin
    SUM := 0 ;
    COUNT := 0 ;
    WRITELN(' Please enter your ',LISTSIZE:1,'-item list.') ;
    while COUNT < LISTSIZE do
        begin
            READ(NUMBER) ;
            SUM := SUM + NUMBER ;
            COUNT := COUNT + 1 ;
        end ;
    WRITELN(' The average is ',SUM/COUNT)
end.
```

The program would be more flexible if it could be used with lists of different sizes. One way to allow this would be to request the value of LISTSIZE using a READ statement. This approach, however, has a drawback: it requires the user to count the number of items in the list.

An alternate solution would be to set aside one value to act as a "stop code." If we knew in advance that -1 would never occur in the list, for example, we could use -1 to indicate the end of the list. With this approach, the first value of NUMBER must be read before the while loop; otherwise, NUMBER will be undefined when the while test is first made. Example 5.4 shows how the revised program might look.

EXAMPLE 5.4:   Terminating input with a stop code


```
program AVERAGE4(INPUT,OUTPUT) ;
const
    STOPCODE = -1 ;
var
    SUM,NUMBER : REAL ;
    COUNT : INTEGER ;
begin
    SUM := 0 ;
    COUNT := 0 ;
    WRITELN(' Please enter the list, terminating it') ;
    WRITELN(' with ',STOPCODE:1) ;
    READ(NUMBER) ;
    while NUMBER < > STOPCODE do
        begin
            SUM := SUM + NUMBER ;
            COUNT := COUNT + 1 ;
            READ(NUMBER)
        end ;
    WRITELN(' The average is ',SUM/COUNT)
end.
```

The program is now more flexible, because the user doesn't have to know the size of the list in advance. Pascal provides a boolean function, EOF(INPUT), that lets us check for the end of input without setting aside a stop code value. EOF stands for End-Of-File. When there is no input left, EOF returns the boolean value TRUE; as long as more input data remains, EOF returns the boolean value FALSE. EOF is valid only if the most recent input operation was READLN. To use EOF in the averaging program, change the READs in Example 5.4 to READLNs, and replace the while statement with this one:

```
while not EOF(INPUT) do
```

When a program malfunctions, the cause of the malfunction often lies in the design of a loop. One common cause of program malfunction is an infinite loop. An infinite loop is a loop that never stops. Infinite loops are usually the result of errors in program logic, rather than syntax errors. The following loop will continue indefinitely because the programmer forgot to have

COUNT incremented:

```
SUM := 0 ;
COUNT := 0 ;
while COUNT < LISTSIZE do
     begin
          READ(NUMBER) ;
          SUM := SUM + NUMBER
     end ;
```

An infinite loop arises when a loop has been constructed in such a way that the condition tested never becomes false. Some infinite loops are the result of simple carelessness, as in the preceding example. More often, however, they are caused by the programmer's inadequate understanding of the program.

Problem Set

*1.   Assuming that DUMMY has been assigned a value, what will happen when the statement below is encountered?

```
while DUMMY = DUMMY do
     WRITELN('*')
```

*2.   The if statement below will yield an arithmetic error when X<0. Using nested ifs, rewrite the statement so that LN(X) is not evaluated when X≤0.

```
if (X>0) and (LN(X) >= 0) then
     WRITELN(' X to the Y power equals ',
          EXP(Y*LN(X)):5)
```

3.   Why will the following statement sequence eventually yield an overflow error?

```
COUNT := 0;
while COUNT = MAXINT do
     COUNT := COUNT + 1
```

4.   Write a program that accepts temperature read ings (in degrees Centigrade) from the user. For each temperature, the program should produce output indicating whether the temperature is below, equal to, or above freezing. After all the temperatures have been read, the program should print the num-

ber of temperatures in the list, the highest temperature read, and the lowest temperature read.

*5. Write a program that accepts an integer and determines whether it is a prime number.

6

Are you a considerate programmer?

6.1 THE PEOPLE YOU SHOULD BE CONSIDERATE OF

How often are you called upon to write for other people? Probably quite frequently. Most of the things you write--memos, letters, research papers, and so forth--are intended for consumption by other people.

When you write for others, you are probably careful to use good grammatical style: not merely because it is expected of you, but also because it makes your writing easier to understand. In short, good style makes you a better communicator. When you write carelessly and incoherently, you are showing a lack of regard for your reader.

A computer program is a work of writing, too. Most programs are read and used by many people besides their original programmers. As a consequence, the programmer who writes muddled, undecipherable programs is really showing the same inconsideration as the author who produces convoluted paragraphs.

Programming style, then, is more than just a set of rules to be followed blindly: it is an exercise in communication. When you write a program, you should try to be considerate of three

people. The first is the person who will use your
program. The user of a program, like the reader
of a book, wants information presented in a clear
and easily digested form. As we discussed in
Chapter 3, it is unreasonable--and unnecessary--
to subject users to poorly designed output.

In this context, the term output refers not
only to the report of the final results, but also
to the intermediate output that guides the user
through the program. One important function of
this intermediate output is to request input data
from the user. The messages that a program uses
to request input are called prompting messages.
As with other types of output, prompting messages
should be carefully designed to minimize the likelihood of confusion.

The second person you should be considerate
of is the programmer who will someday want to read
your program. Other programmers might want to
read your program for any number of reasons. They
might want to incorporate the algorithm you used
into another program, for example. Or, they might
want to enhance your program with a new feature
of their own. In either case, they will be
grateful if you have written your program in a
straightforward and comprehensible way.

The third person you should be considerate
of is yourself. Even if no one else ever uses
or examines your completed program, the effort
you put into making the program comprehensible
will still pay off. It will pay off because,
as your programs become more complex, you will
be left with more design details to contend with.
If you use good programming style from the start,
these design details will be far easier to keep
straight.

6.2 DOs AND DON'Ts FOR CONSIDERATE PROGRAMMERS

Although programming style is largely a matter of
common sense, some elements of style are so essential that they are worth memorizing. The DOs and
DON'Ts that follow are not meant to be confining
straitjackets: they are simply guidelines to
help you write better programs. If you use them
consistently, alongside your own common sense,
you will find your programs both easier to read
and easier to use.

Do use descriptive identifiers. If you have
a variable for gross pay information, don't give
it a meaningless name like X1 or ABC--just call
it GROSSPAY. A programmer, like an author, must
strive to communicate. The best way to communicate the meaning of a variable or a symbolic
constant is to give it a name that reflects its
purpose.

Do use indenting to indicate program structure.
In this book, the sample programs are indented so
that each level of nesting is clearly distinguish-
able. The action statement (or compound statement) of an if is set off a few spaces, as is the
action statement of a while loop. On some computers, this formatting is handled automatically
by a special program called a prettyprinter. If
you don't have a prettyprinter available, try
to follow the indenting form used in the sample
programs.

Do write prompting messages in plain English.
A prompting message doesn't have to be a literary
masterpiece, but it should at least be understand-
able. Some programmers, unfortunately, feel com-
pelled to clutter their prompting messages with
cryptic abbreviations and confusing diction.
Resist those temptations. The ideal prompt is
both unambiguous and unintimidating; in short,
it is one that communicates well.

Don't use a variable for more than one purpose.
Once you have declared a variable, you might be
inclined to squeeze extra mileage from it by using
it for different things in different sections of
the program. After you have finished using GROSS-
PAY to store gross pay, for instance, you might
want to reuse it later in the program as a loop
counter. Is this a worthwhile savings?
    The answer is "no." If you reuse GROSSPAY,
all you will save is the trivial inconvenience
of declaring another variable. Furthermore,
this corner-cutting will be accompanied by a
significant decrease in program readability.
What good is a descriptive name like GROSSPAY if
the variable is also going to masquerade as a
loop counter? You may be able to keep track of
GROSSPAY's multiple identities when you first
write the program, but if you decide to modify
it someday, you will be faced with the needless
task of sorting them out again.

Don't use multiple statements per line. In Pascal you are allowed to put more than one statement on a single line. This practice should be avoided, however, because it obscures program structure. For instance, the program shown in Example 6.1 is the same as the one presented in Example 5.3.

EXAMPLE 6.1: An unreadable program

```
program SQUISHED(INPUT,OUTPUT) ; const LISTSIZE = 10 ;
var SUM,NUMBER : REAL ; COUNT : INTEGER ;
begin SUM := 0 ; COUNT := 0 ; WRITELN
(' Please enter your ',LISTSIZE:3,'-item list.') ; while
COUNT<LISTSIZE do begin READ(NUMBER) ; SUM :=
SUM+NUMBER ; COUNT := COUNT + 1 end ;
WRITELN(' The average is ',SUM/COUNT) end.
```

You probably couldn't make this program much harder to read than it is now. In comparison with the original program, which is conveniently indented to emphasize nested logic, the compacted version has no redeeming qualities. When you make several statements run together on a single line, you are creating an unncessary obstacle to readability.

Don't scrounge for efficiencies. From time to time you may run across an "efficiency suggestion" in a computer textbook, a magazine article, or wherever. Invariably these suggestions urge you to shave a few milliseconds off your programs with some recondite trick. Not only do these tricks have a miniscule effect on efficiency, but they also entail a substantial sacrifice in readability. On balance, they are best forgotten.
Efficiency is not, in itself, a bad thing. Unfortunately, the quest for efficient coding is easily taken to extremes. An excessive concern for program efficiency will cause a far more important goal--program readability--to go neglected.

6.3 USING COMMENTS TO CLARIFY

Another way to communicate in a program is to spice the program with comments. A comment is a text that is inserted in a program to clarify the programmer's intentions. Comments are ignored by the computer; they have no effect on program execution. Their purpose is to make the program easier for a human reader to understand.

EXAMPLE 6.2:   Compounding interest

```
program COMPOUND(INPUT,OUTPUT) ;

(* This program calculates the return on a time
   deposit, with interest compounded annually.  *)

var
   AMOUNT : REAL ;        (* Amount of money *)
   INTEREST : REAL ;      (* Annual rate of return *)
   TIME : INTEGER ;       (* Number of years *)

begin
   (*  -- Request the principal, interest, and duration -- *)
   WRITELN(' What is the amount of the principal? ') ;
   READ(AMOUNT) ;
   WRITELN(' What is the percentage interest rate? ') ;
   READ(INTEREST) ;
   INTEREST := INTEREST/100 ;   (* Convert percentage to
                                        decimal *)
   WRITELN(' How many years is the interest paid? ') ;
   READ(TIME) ;

   (*  -- Compute the final amount --  *)
   while TIME > 0 do
      begin
        AMOUNT := AMOUNT * (1+INTEREST) ;
        TIME := TIME - 1
      end ;

   (*   -- Report the results --   *)
   WRITELN(' The final amount is ',AMOUNT:9:2)
end
```

Example 6.2 shows how comments can be used. Anything enclosed by the symbols (* and *) is treated as a comment. There are no restrictions on the length or contents of a comment: they can include numbers, letters, and even reserved words. They can be inserted anywhere in a program, except in the middle of a word or a number.

The comments used in the example can be placed into four classifications. The first is the comment beneath the header that explains what the program is for. The second consists of the comments that summarize the purpose of each constant and each variable. The third consists of the comments that divide the program into paragraph-like groups of related statements. The fourth consists of the comments that explain unusual or nonobvious aspects of the algorithm being used.

There is no universally accepted convention to determine where you should insert comments. As you would expect, usage of comments is dictated primarily by personal taste. The commenting style in Example 6.2 is a good model, though, because it answers most of the questions that someone is likely to raise: What does the program do? What is this variable for? What is the purpose of that statement? In short, what is the programmer trying to accomplish?

7

More conditional statements

7.1   MORE ON LOOPING

As we have seen, the _while_ statement is one way
to create a loop. When a _while_ is encountered,
the computer tests the specified boolean condition. If the condition is true, the action part
of the _while_ is executed repetitively as long as
the condition remains true. If the condition is
initially false, the action is not executed at
all.
     What if we want to create a loop whose
action is executed _at least_ once? That is what
the _repeat...until_ statement is for.

     A _repeat_ loop is constructed slightly differ-
ently from a _while_ loop: to form a _repeat_ loop
involving more than one statement, it is
unnecessary to bracket the statement sequence
with _begin_ and _end_. The reserved words _repeat_
and _until_ act as compound statement brackets on
their own. Example 7.1 shows a program that uses
a _repeat_ loop.

REPEAT...UNTIL

General form: repeat
                             statement list
                 until condition

Repeat...until works like a while loop. The difference is that
while tests the condition before performing the action, whereas
repeat tests the condition after performing the action. This
guarantees that, in a repeat loop, the action is performed at
least once before the loop is terminated.

Examples:

```
repeat
     READ(NUMBER)  ;
     SUM := SUM+NUMBER
until NUMBER = -1

repeat
     COUNT := COUNT+1 ;
     WRITELN(SQR(COUNT))
until COUNT = 25
```

EXAMPLE 7.1:   Prime numbers


```
program PRIME(INPUT,OUTPUT) ;

(*  This program determines whether a number is prime.  *)

var
     NUMBER : INTEGER ;        (* Object of test *)
     COUNT : INTEGER ;         (* Possible divisors *)

begin
     (*  --Get the number to be tested --  *)
     WRITELN(' What number is to be tested? ') ;
     READ(NUMBER) ;

     (* -- Is it prime? --  *)
     COUNT := 1 ;
     repeat
        COUNT := COUNT + 1
     until NUMBER mod COUNT = 0 ;

     (* -- Report the results --  *)
     if COUNT = NUMBER then
        WRITELN(NUMBER,' is prime.')
     else
        WRITELN(NUMBER,' is divisible by ',COUNT)
end.
```

This program uses a <u>repeat</u> loop to determine whether a number is prime. Using the <u>mod</u> operator, it tests each integer between 2 and NUMBER to see if it is a factor of NUMBER. If a factor is found, the loop terminates with COUNT equal to the factor. If NUMBER is prime, the loop ends with COUNT equal to NUMBER. (The loop will not become an infinite loop, because a number is always divisible by itself.)

The program in Example 7.2 has a flaw. This flaw will cause the program to produce incorrect results. Can you see why?

EXAMPLE 7.2: One <u>way</u> <u>to</u> <u>misuse</u> <u>repeat</u>

```
program BADPROG(INPUT,OUTPUT) ;

(* This program reads a list of numbers and finds their
   average.  The end of the list should be marked with
   a stop code of -1.  *)

const
    STOPCODE = -1 ;            (* End-of-list marker *)
var
    SUM : REAL ;               (* Sum of list *)
    NUMBER : REAL ;            (* Last number read *)
    COUNT : INTEGER ;          (* Size of list *)

begin
    (*  -- Output a prompting message --  *)
    SUM := 0 ;
    COUNT := 0 ;
    WRITELN(' Please enter the list, terminating it' ;
    WRITELN(' with ',STOPCODE:1) ;

    (*  -- Read the list --  *)
    repeat
       READ(NUMBER) ;
       SUM := SUM+NUMBER ;
       COUNT := COUNT+1
    until NUMBER = STOPCODE ;

    (*  -- Print the average --  *)
    WRITELN(' The average is ',SUM/COUNT)
end.
```

The program, a modified version of Example 5.4, will not work because the loop was badly designed. When the value of STOPCODE is detected in the list

the loop will terminate as it is supposed to.
Before terminating, however, the loop will cause
STOPCODE to be added to SUM. Here is a better way
to write the loop:

```
repeat
     READ(NUMBER) ;
     if NUMBER < > STOPCODE then
          begin
               SUM := SUM+NUMBER ;
               COUNT := COUNT+1
          end
until NUMBER = STOPCODE :
```

To prevent similar flaws from creeping into
your programs, be especially careful in designing
loops. Watch for errors in both loop preparation
and loop termination. If you don't, you can
expect loop errors to be a frequent cause of program failure.

7.2 COUNTED LOOPS

A counted loop is one designed to repeat a
predetermined number of times. Example 5.3, for
instance, uses a counted loop to read a list whose
size is known in advance. Loops of this kind are
used so often that Pascal provides a special control structure for them.

FOR...TO
FOR...DOWNTO

General forms:
     for control variable := initial value to final value do
          statement

     for control variable := initial value downto final value do
          statement

When a for statement is encountered, the control variable
is set equal to the specified initial value. The action statement (or compound statement) is then executed repetitively.
Each time the action statement is executed, the control
variable is incremented by +1 (for...to) or decremented by
-1 (for...downto). The loop terminates after the control
variable reaches the final value.

Examples:

```
            for COUNT := 1 to LISTSIZE do
                begin
                    READ(NUMBER) ;
                    SUM := SUM + NUMBER
                end

            for LENGTH := 15 downto 1 do
                WRITELN(SQR(LENGTH))

            for MULTI := 1 to 10 do
                for MULT2 := 1 to 10 do
                    WRITELN(MULTI,' times ',MULT2,' equals,'
                    MULTI*MULT2)

            for RANGE := LOWER+1 to UPPER*3
                WRITELN(SQRT(RANGE))
```

You can set up a counted loop with a <u>while</u> or a <u>repeat</u>, but this new structure is easier to use. When you use <u>for</u>, the computer does some of the dirty work for you: it automatically initializes the control variable and increments (or decrements) the control variable for every repetition. The only restriction is that the control variable must not be of type REAL.

The action part of a <u>for</u> loop can be a single statement or a compound statement. If the initial value of a <u>for</u>...<u>to</u> loop is greater than the final value, the action is not executed at all. Thus, the following statement will have no effect:

```
            for COUNT := 1 to 0 do
                WRITELN(COUNT)
```

This loop, however, will print the integers from one to ten:

```
            for COUNT := 1 to 10 do
                WRITELN(COUNT)
```

The next loop, as you might guess, counts down from ten to one:

```
            for COUNT := 10 downto 1 do
                WRITELN(COUNT)
```

The action part of a <u>for</u> loop is often another <u>for</u> loop. An arrangement of this sort is called a <u>nested</u> loop. Each time the innermost loop is completed, the control variable of the outer loop is incremented. This repetition continues until the outer loop is completed. The following nested loop will print pairs of numbers, starting with (1,1), (1,2), (1,3) and ending with (10,10):

```
for LENGTH := 1 to 10 do
    for WIDTH := 1 to 10 do
        WRITELN(LENGTH,WIDTH)
```

The control variable of a <u>for</u> loop cannot be modified by the statements within the loop. It can be accessed and used in calculations, but it cannot be assigned a new value; only the loop mechanism itself can do that. Thus, the loop below is invalid:

```
for COUNT := 1 to 10 do
    begin
        .
        .
        .
        COUNT := COUNT - 1
    end
```

You must declare a control variable, just as you would any other variable. Control variables are usually of type INTEGER, but in a later chapter we will discuss some other data types that cam be used to index a <u>for</u> loop. In the interim, remember that control variables cannot be of type REAL.

What is the value of a control variable after its loop has been terminated? It seems reasonable to assume that it would be equal to the final value specified by the <u>for</u>...<u>to</u> statement. In practice, that's not always the case. In this fragment, for instance, the WRITELN following the loop will not necessarily print the value 10:

```
for COUNT := -10 to 10 do
    WRITELN(SQR(COUNT)) ;
WRITELN(COUNT)
```

Within the loop, COUNT will take the expected values -10, -9,..., +9, +10. Immediately after the loop, however, COUNT could be equal to 10 or 11, depending on the specific version of Pascal you are using. This is simply a quirk of the <u>for</u> statement. As a consequence, you should not use the value of a control variable outside its loop.

7.3   MULTIPLE CONDITION BRANCHING

The if statement allows program flow to branch on
the result of a boolean condition. Using multiple
ifs, we can construct branches involving multiple
conditions. The following fragment shows how a
series of ifs could be used to convert an integer
(in the range 0-9) into word form.

```
if DIGIT = 0 then
     WRITELN(' zero') ;
if DIGIT ¯ 1 then
     WRITELN(' one') ;
          .
          .
          .
```

This approach is rather longwinded.   Pascal
provides   another   control   structure,   the   case
statement, that lets us construct multiple condition branches in a more readable way.

```
CASE

General form:  case expression of
                   values : statement ;
                   values : statement ;
                              :
                   values : statement
          end
```

When a case statement is encountered, the specified
expression is evaluated. The statement (or compound
statement) corresponding to the result of the expression is then executed.

Examples:
```
    case NUMBER mod 2 of
         0 : WRITELN(NUMBER,' is even.') ;
         1 : WRITELN(NUMBER,' is odd.')
    end

    case MONTH of
         1,2,3 : WRITELN(' First quarter') ;
         4,5,6 : WRITELN(' Second quarter') ;
         7,8,9 : WRITELN(' Third quarter') ;
         10,11,12: WRITELN(' Fourth quarter')
    end
```

```
    case CODE of
        1 : for COUNT := 1 to 5 do
            WRITELN(' ') ;
        2 : begin
            WRITELN(' ') ;
            WRITELN('-------------------')
            end ;
        3 :
    end
```

Like the control variable of a <u>for</u> statement, the selector of a <u>case</u> statement must have a non-real type. The selector can be any expression. For each possible value of the selector, there must be one (and only one) corresponding entry in the statement list. Thus, if ORDER equals 5, the following <u>case</u> statement will cause an error:

```
    case ORDER OF
        0 : WRITELN(' No readings have been
                    taken.') ;
        1 : WRITELN(' This is the first
                    reading.') ;
        2 : ;
        3,4 : WRITELN(' This is reading number ',
                    ORDER)
    end
```

Notice that the entry for ORDER=2 does not specify a statement. What happens, then, when ORDER equals 2? In effect, the entry for ORDER=2 is a <u>null</u> statement. When ORDER equals 2, no special action is taken.

Example 7.3 illustrates a simple application for the <u>case</u> statement. The program uses an <u>if</u> to ensure that the <u>case</u> selector, DIGIT, is within the expected range. If the user accidentally enters an improper value, a brief error message will be printed.

7.4   EXCEPTIONAL TRANSFER

The control structures that we have discussed so far will be adequate 99.9 percent of the time. For every selective or iterative process that you might want to define, one of these control structures will do the job. Nevertheless, Pascal

---

EXAMPLE 7.3: Converting digits into words

```
program DIGITS(INPUT,OUTPUT) ;

(*  This program accepts an integer in the range 0-9 and
    prints it in word form.  *)

var
    DIGIT : INTEGER ;              (* User input *)

begin
    WRITELN(' Please enter a single digit.') ;
    READ(DIGIT) ;
    if (DIGIT < 0) or (DIGIT > 9)  then
      WRITELN(' This number is outside the range 0-9.')
    else
      begin
        WRITE(' The word form of this digit is ') ;
        case DIGIT of
          0 : WRITELN('zero') ;
          1 : WRITELN('one') ;
          2 : WRITELN('two') ;
          3 : WRITELN('three') ;
          4 : WRITELN('four') ;
          5 : WRITELN('five') ;
          6 : WRITELN('six') ;
          7 : WRITELN('seven') ;
          8 : WRITELN('eight') ;
          9 : WRITELN('nine')
        end
      end
end.
```

---

additionally provides a facility for performing exceptional transfers.

An exceptional transfer causes program flow to jump, unconditionally, from one location in the program to another. To place an exceptional transfer in a program, you must do three things. First, you must give the transfer destination a numeric "label," like this:

        999: end

This end statement now has the label 999. (Labels always go at the beginning of a statement.) Next, you must declare the label at the beginning of the program, like this:

label 999 ;

(Label declarations go between the program header and the constant declarations.) Finally, you must insert a goto statement at the program location where the transfer is to originate. A goto causes program flow to jump to the statement with the specified label. You can insert a goto statement anyplace you would insert any other statement. For example:

```
if THETA = 360 then
     goto 999
else
     WRITELN(' The figure is not a circle.')
```

When must one use an exceptional transfer? The answer is "never." Any program written with gotos can also be written without gotos. Strictly speaking, the goto statement is superfluous.

When should one use an exceptional transfer? This is the more important question, but it is also more difficult to answer. In general, exceptional transfers are justified only in two circumstances: to terminate a for loop prematurely or to terminate the program prematurely. Even then, one of the standard control structures will usually serve equally well.

Don't be surprised if you almost never have an occasion to use exceptional transfers. You should avoid them, in fact, because they reduce program readability. Carelessly used, the goto statement can complicate a program so much that the flow of control becomes tortuously difficult to predict.

Problem Set

*1. How many times will the following loop be repeated?

```
for COUNT := 1 downto 10 do
     WRITELN(COUNT)
```

 2. Write a program to accept an integer ≥ 2 from the user. The program should use a loop to find the sum of all the integers between 1 and the user's number. In other words, if the number is $\underline{n}$, then your program should calculate:

$$\sum_{k=1}^{n} k \qquad \text{or} \qquad 1+2+3...+(n-1)+n$$

3. Suppose the colors blue, red, and green are
    represented by the integer values 1, 2, and
    3, respectively. Write three program frag-
    ments that will print "BLUE," "RED," or
    "GREEN," based on the value of the integer
    variable COLOR. The first fragment should
    use nested ifs; the second should use a
    sequence of unnested ifs; and the third
    should use a case statement.

*4. Rewrite Example 5.3 using a for loop.

*5. How many times will the WRITELN be executed
     in the nested loop below?

```
for COUNT1 := 1 to 4 do
    for COUNT2 := 1 to 8 do
        WRITELN(COUNT1*COUNT2)
```

8

Defining your own data types

8.1 ENUMERATED TYPES

So far we have examined three data types: REAL,
INTEGER, and BOOLEAN. With these types, we can
store floating point numbers like 3.1415 or 2.718,
integers like 152 or -3, and the boolean values
true and false. At times, however, we will be
working with data that doesn't fit neatly into any
of these categories.

Suppose you wanted to keep track of the months
of the year. If you were restricted to using
Pascal's built-in types, you might devise a scheme
where the integer 0 stands for January, 1 for Feb-
ruary, 2 for March, and so on. To give THISMONTH
the value "June," you would then write

        THISMONTH := 5

Obviously, this contrivance is a bit incon-
venient. It forces us to make the mental effort
of keeping the numerical codes straight. What you
really want to write is

        THISMONTH := JUNE

What you want to do, in other words, is create a brand-new data type. Pascal lets you do just that. The declaration below defines two variables --THISMONTH and LASTMONTH--whose values may be months of the year:

```
THISMONTH,LASTMONTH : (JAN,FEB,MARCH,APRIL,
                       MAY,JUNE,JULY,AUG,SEPT,
                       OCT,NOV,DEC)
```

Now we have created a new type composed of the values enumerated in the parentheses. This is an example of an enumerated type. An enumerated type is a programmer-defined type composed of a set of enumerated elements. Here are some more declarations that create enumerated types:

```
SUNSIGN : (AQUARIUS,PISCES,ARIES,TAURUS,
           GEMINI,CANCER,LEO,VIRGO,LIBRA,
           SCORPIO,SAGITTARIUS,CAPRICORN)
TODAY : (SUNDAY,MONDAY,TUESDAY,WEDNESDAY,
         THURSDAY,FRIDAY,SATURDAY)
SEX  : (MALE,FEMALE)
```

It may seem strange to think of a variable representing a month. Yet that is exactly what THISMONTH and LASTMONTH are doing. A variable of an enumerated type may be assigned any "value" within its type. In a program where SUNSIGN has been declared as it is above, we could write assignment statements like this:

```
SUNSIGN := PISCES
```

Variables with enumerated types can also be used in boolean expressions, just like other variables:

```
if THISMONTH = OCT then
   WRITELN(' October.')
```

The other relational operators can be used, too:

```
if THISMONTH > SEPT then
    WRITELN(' Fourth quarter.')
```

An interesting question arises here: how can one element of an enumerated type be greater than or less than another? In other words, how can FEB be greater than or less than SEPT? The answer lies in the ordering of the elements in the declaration. Enumerating a data type automatically establishes a relational order among the elements. The leftmost element in the declaration is the minimum value, and the rightmost is the maximum value. For TODAY, this means that

SUNDAY < MONDAY < ... < FRIDAY < SATURDAY

Variables with enumerated types can be incorporated into any of Pascal's control structures. Here is a <u>for</u> statement that "counts" from SEPT to DEC:

```
for LASTMONTH := SEPT to DEC do
    begin
        .
        .
        .
    end
```

Within the loop, LASTMONTH takes the successive values SEPT, OCT, NOV, and DEC. Here is a <u>case</u> statement whose selector is a variable of an enumerated type:

```
case THISMONTH of
 JAN,FEB,MARCH : WRITELN(' First quarter.') ;
 APRIL,MAY,JUNE : WRITELN(' Second quarter.');
 JULY,AUG,SEPT : WRITELN(' Third quarter.') ;
 OCT,NOV,DEC : WRITELN(' Fourth quarter.')
end
```

The elements of an enumerated type are governed by the naming rules that apply to variables and symbolic constants. They cannot start with a non-alphabetic character, for example, and they cannot contain any character that is not a letter or a digit. They cannot be reserved words, either. Thus, the following declaration is invalid:

DUMMY : (3STAR,HELLO?,BEGIN)

It is also important to remember that all identifiers in a Pascal program must be unique. In other words, all variables, symbolic constants, and enumeration elements must have different names. A variable cannot have the same name as a symbolic constant, obviously, because there would be no way to tell them apart. Likewise, the name of an enumeration element must not conflict with any other identifiers in the program. For this reason, the following declarations would be rejected if they appeared in the same program:

BLUE : INTEGER ;
COLOR : (RED,GREEN,BLUE) ;

8.2 SUBRANGE TYPES

Suppose you wanted to keep track of the number of days that a person reported for work in a certain week. You might declare a variable, DAYSWORKED, of type INTEGER. If the person did not come to work at all, DAYSWORKED would be set to zero. At the other extreme, if the person worked every day, DAYSWORKED would be set to seven.

For occasions like this, Pascal provides subrange types. A subrange type is a fragment of some other type, called the host type. Here is a declaration that creates a variable with a subrange type:

DAYSWORKED : 0..7

The ellipsis notation specifies the lower and upper bounds of the subrange. In the preceding declaration, the host type is INTEGER. DAYSWORKED can now be used like an ordinary integer variable, with one exception: it cannot be given a value outside the subrange 0..7. That is, it cannot be less than zero or greater than seven. If it is given a value outside this range, an error condition will result.

The host type cannot be the type REAL. The host type can, however, be an enumerated type. Assuming that TODAY has been declared as in section 8.1, for example, the following declaration would create a subrange whose host type is (SUNDAY,MONDAY,TUESDAY,WEDNESDAY,THURSDAY,FRIDAY, SATURDAY).

WEEKDAY : MONDAY..FRIDAY

The upper and lower bounds of a subrange can be specified with either literal constants (like -1 or 16) or symbolic constants (like LISTSIZE or STOPCODE). To illustrate the use of symbolic con-

stants in this situation, here is a sequence of
declarations from a hypothetical program:

```
const
      MINVALUE = -10 ;        (* lower bound *)
      MAXVALUE = 25 ;         (* upper bound *)
var
      NUMBER : MINVALUE..MAXVALUE ;
```

NUMBER is now an integer variable that can
take values in the subrange -10 to 25. The use of
symbolic constants in subrange definitions is a
common practice, especially when the subrange
bounds are obscure or nonobvious.

EXAMPLE 8.1:   Checking For Leap Years

```
program LEAPYEAR(INPUT,OUTPUT) ;

(*   This program accepts a Gregorian year from the
     user.  It will then determine whether the year
     is a leap year.    *)

var
     YEAR : 1582..9999 ;
     EXTRADAY : BOOLEAN ;

begin
     (*  -- Get the year --  *)
     WRITELN(' What year do you want tested? ') ;
     READ(YEAR) ;

     (*  -- Is it a leap year? --  *)
     EXTRADAY := FALSE ;
     if (YEAR mod 4 = 0) and (YEAR mod 100 <> 0)  then
       EXTRADAY := TRUE ;
     if YEAR mod 400 = 0  then
       EXTRADAY := TRUE ;

     (*  -- Report the results --  *)
     if EXTRADAY then
       WRITELN(YEAR:4,' is a leap year.')
     else
       WRITELN(YEAR:4,' is not a leap year.')
end
```

The program in Example 8.1 gives YEAR a subrange type with a lower bound of 1582 and an upper

bound of 9999. If the user enters a number outside this subrange, an error message is printed
and the program halts. If the user enters a valid
number, the program tests it to determine whether
it represents a leap year.

Subrange types are useful for two reasons.
First, they can enhance program readability. When
you specify the possible values that a variable
can have, you are supplying helpful information
about the purpose of the variable. Second, the
error messages that report out-of-range conditions
can alert you to previously undetected bugs in the
program logic.

8.3   TYPE DECLARATIONS

There are two ways to define a new data type in
Pascal. The first way is to define the type within the variable declaration itself. This is the
method we have used so far. To create a variable
called COLOR with an enumerated type, you could
write a declaration like this:

    COLOR : (RED,GREEN,BLUE)

There is also a second way to define a data
type. If you like, you can declare a data
type separately and give it a name. Here is a
type declaration that creates a data type named
PALETTE:

    PALETTE = (RED,GREEN,BLUE)

PALETTE is now a type indentifier, just like
INTEGER and BOOLEAN. Type declarations go between
the constant and variable declarations. Assuming
that PALETTE has been declared as above, you could
write a variable declaration like this one:

    COLOR : PALETTE

COLOR is now a variable of type (RED,GREEN,
BLUE). Notice that a type declaration uses an
equals sign rather than a colon. The type
declarations in a program are preceded by the
reserved word type.

EXAMPLE 8.2:   Declaring A Data Type

```
program LEAP2(INPUT,OUTPUT) ;

(*   This program accepts a Gregorian year from the user.
     It will then determine whether the year is a leap year.   *)

type
    GREGORIAN = 1582..9999 ;
var
    YEAR : GREGORIAN ;
    EXTRADAY : BOOLEAN ;

begin
    (* -- Get the year --  *)
    WRITELN(' What year do you want tested? ') ;
    READ(YEAR) ;

    (* -- Is it a leap year? --  *)
    EXTRADAY := FALSE ;
    if (YEAR mod 4 = 0) and (YEAR mod 100 <> 0) then
        EXTRADAY := TRUE ;
    if YEAR mod 400 = 0 then
        EXTRADAY := TRUE ;

    (* -- Report the results --  *)
    if EXTRADAY then
        WRITELN(YEAR:4,' is a leap year.')
    else
        WRITELN(YEAR:4,' is not a leap year.')
end.
```

The program shown in Example 8.2 is a revised version of Example 8.1. It declares the type GREGORIAN to be a subrange of the type INTEGER. The variable YEAR is then declared to be of type GREGORIAN.

8.4   PROPERTIES OF ORDINAL TYPES

With one exception, all the data types we have discussed so far have something in common: they can be expressed as if they were enumerated types. Here is how the built-in types BOOLEAN and INTEGER could be defined:

```
BOOLEAN = (FALSE,TRUE) ;
INTEGER = -MAXINT..MAXINT ;
```

Data types that can be defined this way are called _ordinal_ types. The types BOOLEAN and INTEGER, along with ordinary enumerated types, are ordinal. The type REAL, however, is not.

The distinction between ordinal and non-ordinal types is very important. A variable or an expression used to index a _for_ loop must have an ordinal type; the same is true of a _case_ selector. The host type of a subrange must be ordinal, too.

Except for the minimum and maximum elements, each element of an ordinal type has a _predecessor_ and a _successor_. The integer value 4 has the predecessor 3 and the successor 5. In the enumerated type (JAN,FEB,MARCH,...,NOV,DEC), FEB has the predecessor JAN and the successor MARCH. The minimum element JAN has no predecessor, and the maximum element DEC has no successor. To allow more flexible manipulation of ordinal-type values, Pascal provides the functions PRED and SUCC. These functions accept any ordinal-type expression and return its predecessor or successor. Thus, although it is invalid to write

```
THISMONTH := JAN + 1
```

it is possible to find the element after JAN by writing

```
THISMONTH := SUCC(JAN)
```

Attempting to evaluate undefined expressions like PRED(JAN) or SUCC(DEC) will result in an error condition. You can make an enumerated type appear to "wrap around," however, by using _if_ statements like this one:

```
if THISMONTH = DEC then
    NEXTMONTH := JAN
else
    NEXTMONTH := SUCC(THISMONTH)
```

Each element of an ordinal type also has its own _ordinal number_. For values of type INTEGER (or its subranges), the ordinal number is the value itself. For an enumerated type with n elements, each element has an ordinal number between 0 and n-1. The leftmost element has the

ordinal number 0; the rightmost has the ordinal
number n-1. Pascal provides another function,
ORD, that returns the ordinal number of an
ordinal-type expression. Thus,

```
ORD(100) = 100
ORD(PRED(100)) = 99
ORD(JAN) = 0
ORD(DEC) = 11
ORD(MARCH) = 2
ORD(SUCC(FEB)) = 2
```

Problem Set

*1. Assuming the declarations from Section 8.1,
     which of the following assignments are
     invalid? (COUNT is of type INTEGER.)

```
THISMONTH := MARCH
SUNSIGN := FEMALE
TODAY := ORD(SEX)
SUNSIGN := SUCC(SUNSIGN)
COUNT := ORD(ORD(TODAY))
```

*2. Again assuming the declarations from section
     8.1, which of the following additional
     declarations are invalid?

```
WORKINGDAY : FRIDAY..MONDAY
WHOLE : 0..MAXINT
NEXTMONTH : JAN..DEC
```

 3. Write a program that will accept five semes-
     ter course grades (on a 4.0 scale), along
     with the number of credit hours for each
     course. The program should then print the
     total quality points and the overall average
     for that semester.

 4. First, write a declaration for variable
     SEASON, whose possible values are the four
     seasons. Next, write a program fragment
     that accepts two integers representing a
     day and month, and assigns SEASON the proper
     value based on the specified date.

9
Arrays

9.1 SINGLE-DIMENSION ARRAYS

So far all the data types we have used have been _simple_ types. A simple type is one that can represent only a single value. A variable of type INTEGER, for example, can store one integer number.

Pascal also provides structured types, which can represent a collection of values. The most frequently use fo these types is the array. Here is a variable declaration that creates an array:

```
LIST : array[1..10] of INTEGER
```

Now LIST is an array containing 10 values of type INTEGER. The first component of the array is referred to as LIST[1], the next is LIST[2], and so on. Here is a loop that sets all the components of LIST equal to zero:

```
for COUNT := 1 to 10 do
    LIST[COUNT] := 0
```

The components of array LIST can now be
pictured this way:

```
LIST[1]                    0
LIST[2]                    0
LIST[3]                    0
   .                       .
   .                       .
   .                       .
LIST[10]                   0
```

The values inside the brackets are called
subscripts; they are used to reference specific
components within the array. A subscript can be
any expression. In this example, both the subscripts and the components are of type INTEGER.
Depending on the way an array is declared, however, its components and subscripts may be given
different types.

DECLARING A SINGLE-DIMENSION ARRAY

General form:
    Variable : array[subscript type] of component type

The subscript type must be ordinal. The component
type can be any type.

Examples:
    GRADES : array[1..CLASSSIZE] of REAL
    WEIGHTS : array[0..15] of INTEGER
    MAXTEMPS : array[JAN..DEC] of -20..110

The component type of an array is simply the
data type associated with each of its components.
If an array has the component type INTEGER, for
instance, then each of its components can be used
like an integer variable.
The subscript type defines the range of
possible subscripts. If an attempt is made to
reference a nonexistent component, an error condition will result. Errors of this sort are called
invalid subscript errors. Assuming that LIST has
been declared as above, each of the following statements will yield an invalid subscript error:

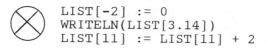

```
LIST[-2] := 0
WRITELN(LIST[3.14])
LIST[11] := LIST[11] + 2
```

If you like to sound sophisticated, you may be interested to know that there is a "correct" method for pronouncing subscript notation. Subscript brackets are pronounced "sub." Thus, to read the term LIST[7] aloud, you would say "list sub seven."

EXAMPLE 9.1:   Tabulating votes

```
program BALLOTS(INPUT,OUTPUT) ;

(*   This program reads a series of ballots, each of which is
     represented by an integer.  The results of the voting will
     then be reported.    *)

const
     STOPCODE = -1 ;          (* Terminates the input *)
     CANDIDATES = 3 ;         (* Number of candidates *)
var
     VOTES : array[1..CANDIDATES] of INTEGER ;
     COUNT : INTEGER ;
     ONEVOTE : INTEGER ;

begin
     (*  -- Everyone starts with zero votes --  *)
     for COUNT := 1 to CANDIDATES do
          VOTES[COUNT] := 0 ;

     (*  -- Read the ballots --  *)
     WRITELN(' Each ballot should be represented by a') ;
     WRITELN(' number between 1 and ',CANDIDATES:1,'.') ;
     WRITELN(' Please enter the ballots, terminating the') ;
     WRITELN(' list with the value ',STOPCODE:2,'.') ;
     READ(ONEVOTE) ;
     while ONEVOTE <> STOPCODE do
        begin
          if (ONEVOTE 1) or (ONEVOTE CANDIDATES) then
             WRITELN(' A ballot marked ',ONEVOTE,' was
                     discarded.')
          else
             VOTES[ONEVOTE] := VOTES[ONEVOTE] + 1 ;
          READ(ONEVOTE)
        end ;
```

```
        (*   -- Report the outcome --   *)
        WRITELN(' ') ;
        WRITELN(' The results of the voting are as follows: ') ;
        WRITELN(' ') ;
        for COUNT := 1 to CANDIDATES do
           WRITELN(' Candidate #',COUNT:2,' received ',
                   VOTES [COUNT],' votes ')
   end.
```

The program shown in Example 9.1 uses an array to tally the votes cast in an election. Each component of VOTES contains the total number of ballots received by a certain candidate. VOTES[1] contains the number of ballots for candidate #1, VOTES[2] contains the number of ballots for candidate #2, and so on. If the program reads a value outside the expected range, a message is printed and the ballot is discarded.

Since the subscript type of an array is often a subrange type (such as 1..10 or JAN..DEC), it is possible to specify subscript bounds with symbolic constants. In this example, the identifier CANDIDATES is a symbolic constant declared to equal 3. To change the number of candidates in the race, you would need to change only the constant declaration. (It is not possible, however, to modify the size of an array while a program is running.)

9.2   TYPICAL ARRAY OPERATIONS

Suppose you have an array named ITEMS declared like this:

ITEMS : array[0..63] of REAL

Now, what can you do with it? We have already seen how array components can be assigned values and printed. This usage of arrays, however, only hints at their versatility. Here are some additional array operations that frequently occur:

Searching   Given array LIST as declared above, you might want to know, "How many negative numbers are contained in this array?" Or, perhaps, "Does this array contain the value 2.0?" To answer questions like these, a program would perform a search of the array. Here is a program fragment that searches for the highest value in ITEMS:

```
MAXVALUE := ITEMS[0] ;
for COUNT := 0 to 63 do
      if ITEMS[COUNT] > MAXVALUE then
            MAXVALUE := ITEMS[COUNT] ;
```

MAXVALUE begins with the value of ITEMS[0]. The
for loop then examines each component of ITEMS to
determine whether it contains any larger values.
If a component larger than MAXVALUE is found,
MAXVALUE is updated accordingly. In the end,
then, MAXVALUE will be equal to the largest value
in the array.

Copying   Sometimes it is necessary to copy one
array onto another. If an array called BACKUP
were declared the same way ITEMS was, the following loop would copy all the components of ITEMS
onto their counterparts in BACKUP:

```
for COUNT := 0 to 63 do
      BACKUP[COUNT] := ITEMS[COUNT]
```

The two arrays would now have the same contents. To make this operation simpler, Pascal
allows identically declared arrays to be copied
with one assignment statement. Thus:

```
BACKUP := ITEMS
```

The previous contents of BACKUP would be destroyed
and replaced with the contents of ITEMS. The
array ITEMS itself would not be affected.

Numerical Evaluation   Suppose ITEMS represented
the weekly sales volumes (in dollars) of 64 items
in a company's product line. Given an array of
related numbers like these, you might want to perform a certain numerical evaluation on them. One
possible evaluation would be to sum all the components, arriving at the overall weekly volume of
the product line:

```
WEEKLYVOLUME := 0 ;
for COUNT := 0 to 63 do
  WEEKLYVOLUME := WEEKLYVOLUME + ITEMS[COUNT] ;
```

Another evaluation would be the computation
of a statistical quantity, such as the mean or the
standard deviation. Here is a program fragment
that calculates the mean (i.e., the average) of
the components of ITEMS:

```
SUM := 0 ;
for COUNT := 0 to 63 do
     SUM := SUM + ITEMS[COUNT] ;
MEAN := SUM/64 ;
```

<u>Swapping</u> <u>Components</u>   On some occasions it is
necessary to swap two components of an array. To
<u>swap</u> a pair of components is to exchange their
values: for instance, to give ITEMS[3] the value
of ITEMS[4], and vice-versa. At first glance, the
following statement sequence may appear to perform
a swapping operation:

⊗   ITEMS[3] := ITEMS[4] ;
     ITEMS[4] := ITEMS[3] ;

This won't work. In the end, both ITEMS[3]
and ITEMS[4] will have the same value--namely, the
original value of ITEMS [4]. Here is a statement
sequence that overcomes this difficulty:

```
TEMP := ITEMS[3] ;
ITEMS[3] := ITEMS[4] ;
ITEMS[4] := TEMP ;
```

TEMP is a variable used for temporary storage.
(It presumably has been declared to have the same
type as the component type of ITEMS.) In this
example it is used to preserve the value of
ITEMS[3] during the swapping process.

9.3   MULTI-DIMENSION ARRAYS

Array ITEMS from Section 9.2 is a single-
dimension array. This means that to reference
a specific component of ITEMS, you specify a
single subscript.
     You are not restricted to single-dimension
arrays, however. Arrays can be declared to have
any number of dimensions. The following series
of declarations creates a two-dimensional array:

```
const
  ROWS = 5 ;
  COLUMNS = 7 ;
var
  TABLE : array[1..ROWS,1..COLUMNS] of INTEGER ;
```

A two-dimensional array (like TABLE) is analogous to the mathematical concept of a _matrix_. TABLE has 35 components, each of which is associated with a unique pair of subscripts. Here is a nested loop that sets all the components of TABLE equal to zero:

```
for HEIGHT := 1 to ROWS do
    for WIDTH := 1 to COLUMNS do
        TABLE[HEIGHT,WIDTH] := 0
```

Each time the inner _for_ loop runs its course, the outer loop increments HEIGHT and the inner _for_ loop is repeated. Thus, all the components of TABLE, from TABLE[1,1], TABLE[1,2], TABLE[1,3], etc., through TABLE[5,7] are set equal to zero. The contents of TABLE can now be pictured this way:

	1	2	3	4	5	6	7
1	0	0	0	0	0	0	0
2	0	0	0	0	0	0	0
3	0	0	0	0	0	0	0
4	0	0	0	0	0	0	0
5	0	0	0	0	0	0	0

Both of the subscript types of TABLE are subranges of INTEGER. As with single-dimension arrays, however, a subscript type can be any ordinal type. For example, the following series of declarations is perfectly valid:

```
type
    SUITE = (CLUBS,HEARTS,DIAMONDS,SPADES) ;
    FACEVALUE = 2..14 ;
    DECK = array[SUITE,FACEVALUE] of BOOLEAN ;
var
    DEALT : DECK ;
```

DEALT is now a variable of type DECK. It contains fifty-two components--one for each card in a card deck. Since each component is of type BOOLEAN, you could use the array to keep track of whether or not a particular card has been dealt. To reference the eight of hearts, for instance, you would write DEALT[HEARTS,8]. Here is a program fragment that will print the status of every card:

```
for SUITECOUNT := CLUBS to SPADES do
   for FACECOUNT := 2 to 14 to
      begin
         case SUITECOUNT of
            CLUBS : WRITE(' The ',
                      FACECOUNT:2,
                      ' of clubs') ;
            HEARTS : WRITE(' The ',
                      FACECOUNT:2,' of
                      hearts') ;
            DIAMONDS : WRITE(' The ',
                      FACECOUNT:2,
                      ' of diamonds')
            SPADES : WRITE(' The ',
                      FACECOUNT:2,' of
                      spades')
         end ;
         if DEALT[SUITCOUNT,FACECOUNT] then
            WRITELN(' has been dealt.')
         else
            WRITELN(' has not been dealt.')
      end ;
```

Although we cannot directly visualize arrays
of more than two or three dimensions, it is possible to construct arrays with any number of dimensions. To the computer, a five-dimensional array
works just like a two-dimensional array. As with
one- and two-dimensional arrays, the subscript
types of a five-dimensional array must be ordinal.

9.4   PACKED ARRAYS

There is more than one format that a computer can
use to represent an array inside its memory. Some
formats allow arrays to be stored in less memory
space, but at the cost of slower program execution.
If you like, you can instruct the computer to use
such a format. An array stored in this "tighter"
format is called a packed array. Here is a
declaration that creates a packed array:

    PLAYERS : packed array[1..10] of SCORES

Within the program body, a packed array is
not different from an unpacked array. Any operation that can be performed on an unpacked array
can be performed on a packed array; however, the
operation will be slower on a packed array.

This difference in speed occurs because a component of an unpacked array can be accessed faster than a component of a packed array.

Pascal provides two statements that can be used to copy a packed array onto an unpacked array and vice-versa. Suppose you have arrays PAYROLL and TEMP declared like this:

```
const
      LOWERBOUND = 1 ;
      UPPERBOUND = 10 ;
var
      PAYROLL : array[LOWERBOUND..UPPERBOUND]
            of REAL ;
      TEMP : packed array[LOWERBOUND..
            UPPERBOUND] of REAL ;
```

TEMP is now a packed array and PAYROLL is now an unpacked array. The following statement will copy the contents of PAYROLL onto TEMP, starting with PAYROLL[LOWERBOUND]:

```
PACK(PAYROLL,LOWERBOUND,TEMP)
```

This statement is equivalent to the following loop:

```
for COUNT := LOWERBOUND to UPPERBOUND do
      TEMP[COUNT] := PAYROLL[COUNT]
```

The inverse operation, UNPACK, will copy TEMP onto PAYROLL:

```
UNPACK(TEMP,PAYROLL,LOWERBOUND)
```

When is it best to use a packed array rather than an unpacked array? Most programmers use unpacked arrays as a matter of course, unless they find that a program is occupying too much memory space. A large, infrequently accessed array is then the ideal candidate for packing. Packing a small array yields little savings in memory space; packing a frequently accessed array may slow the program to an unacceptable degree.

Problem Set

*1. Write a type declaration that defines a
     single-dimension array

        --with the subscript type BOOLEAN and the
          component type REAL.
        --with the subscript type HUES and the com-
          ponent type INTEGER.
        --with the subscript type 1..10 and the
          component type 1..10.

*2. Which of the following variable declarations
     are invalid?

     HEIGHTS : array[1..PERSONS] of 5.0 .. 6.9
     STATUS : array[10..1] of BOOLEAN
     VECTOR : array[1..2] of REAL
     SALES : array[10..10,3..3] of INTEGER

 3. Given array ITEMS from section 9.2, write a
     program fragment to reverse all the compo-
     nents of ITEMS. That is, the first and last
     components of ITEMS should be exchanged, the
     second and next-to-last should be exchanged,
     and so on.

 4. Write a program that accepts monthly sales
     figures for a given twelve-month period and
     then identifies

        --the month in which the greatest sales
          increase occurred
        --the month in which the greatest sales
          decrease occurred

10
Data types that represent words

10.1 <u>THE DATA TYPE CHAR</u>

Most computer applications involve alphabetic
information as well as numeric information. A
program designed to maintain mailing lists, for
example, will require a capability for accepting
alphabetic characters as input data, storing them,
and printing them out again. Before we can write
programs that manipulate characters, we will need
a data type to represent them. For this purpose,
Pascal provides the data type CHAR.

Just as a variable of type INTEGER can store
one integer number, a variable of type CHAR can
store a single character. If the variable ALPHA
has been declared to have the type CHAR, then the
following assignments are valid:

```
ALPHA := 'P'
ALPHA := '+'
ALPHA := '3'
ALPHA := ' '
ALPHA := ''''
```

The first assignment sets ALPHA equal to the
character <u>P</u>. The second sets ALPHA equal to the

character +. The third sets ALPHA equal to the character 3̄. (Note that the character 3̄ is distinct from the integer 3. When surrounded by quotation marks, 3̄ is a CHAR value just like any other. Thus, ALPHA could not be used in arithmetic, even though its value happens to represent a numeric digit.)

The fourth assignment sets ALPHA equal to a blank. Although the blank character is not printable, it is still a legal CHAR value. The final assignment sets ALPHA equal to a quotation mark; this is a special case, because quotation marks are used to delimit CHAR values.

The repertoire of CHAR values available on a computer is called the <u>character</u> <u>set</u> of that computer. A typical character set includes the letters of the alphabet, the digits 0-9, and 25 or 30 other symbols. Two common character sets are the American Standard Code for Information Interchange (ASCII) and the Extended Binary Coded Decimal Interchange Code (EBCDIC). The relational ordering among CHAR values is determined by the character set being used. For both ASCII and EBCDIC, the following relations hold:

```
'A' < 'B' < 'C' < ... < 'X' < 'Y' < 'Z'
'0' < '1' < '2' < ... < '7' < '8' < '9'
```

The boolean comparison operators can be used to test equalities and inequalities among CHAR variables. Example 10.1 shows a program that reads two characters and reports whether the first is greater than, equal to, or less than the second.

EXAMPLE <u>10.1</u>: Comparing <u>Two</u> <u>Characters</u>

```
program COMPARE(INPUT,OUTPUT) ;

(*   This program reads two characters.  It will then
     determine whether the first character is greater
     than, equal to, or less than the second.    *)

var
   FIRST,SECOND : CHAR ;    (* input characters *)
```

```
begin
  READ(FIRST,SECOND)  ;
  WRITE(' The first character is ')  ;
  if FIRST > SECOND then
    WRITELN(' greater than the second.')
  else
    if FIRST = SECOND then
      WRITELN(' equal to the second.')
    else
      WRITELN(' less than the second.')
end.
```

Since CHAR is an ordinal type, the functions described in section 8.4 can be used with CHAR values. The SUCC and PRED functions, for instance, return the succeeding and preceding characters in the character set. With ASCII and EBCDIC, SUCC('0') equals '1', because '1' is the character after '0'.

Each character in a character set is associated with a unique integer, called its character code. In ASCII, the character code for 'A' is 65; in EBCDIC, the character code for 'A' is 193. The function ORD returns the character code of any CHAR value. Thus, on a computer that uses ASCII, the expression ORD('A') will equal 65. Similarly, ORD(ALPHA) returns the character code for the present value of ALPHA.

Pascal provides another function, CHR, which accepts an integer argument and returns the corresponding character. On a computer that uses ASCII, then, CHR(65) will equal 'A'. As you might expect, CHR(ORD(ALPHA)) equals ALPHA. Giving CHR an integer that is not a valid character code will result in an error condition.

Unfortunately, standard Pascal does not provide type-transfer functions for converting INTEGER values directly into CHAR values or vice-versa. ORD('3') does not equal 3, and CHR(3) does not equal '3'. It is possible, however, to convert values back and forth. Assuming that COUNT is an integer between 0 and 9 inclusive, you could convert it into a CHAR value with an assignment like this one:

```
ALPHA := CHR(COUNT + ORD('0'))
```

Conversely, if ALPHA contains a numeral character, you could convert it into an INTEGER value by writing

COUNT := ORD(ALPHA) - ORD('0')

The fact CHAR is an ordinal type means that a CHAR variable can be the control variable of a for loop or the selector of a case statement. The following for loop prints all the characters between 'A' and 'Z':

for ALPHA := 'A' to 'Z' do
    WRITE(ALPHA)

The program shown in Example 10.2 uses an array whose subscript type is a subrange of CHAR. The purpose of the program is to find the frequency with which the letters of the alphabet occur in a text. After the program reads the text, each component of the array will contain the number of occurrences recorded for the character that matches its subscript.

EXAMPLE 10.2:   Letter Frequency Distribution

```
program LETTERFREQ(INPUT,OUTPUT) ;

(*  This program reads a text and determines the frequency-
    of-occurrence for each letter.    *)

var
    LETTERS : array['A'..'Z']of INTEGER ;  (* frequencies *)
    TEXT : CHAR ;                    (* input character *)
    INDEX : CHAR ;                   (* loop index *)

begin
(*  -- Read the text --  *)
    while not EOF(INPUT) do
        begin
            READ(TEXT) ;
            if  (TEXT > =  'A') and (TEXT < = 'Z') then
                LETTERS[TEXT] := LETTERS[TEXT] + I
        end  ;

(*  -- Print the results --  *)
    WRITELN(' Character      Frequency')  ;
    for INDEX := 'A' to 'Z' do
        WRITELN(INDEX,LETTERS[INDEX]:15))
end.
```

Like other data types, the type CHAR can be used in a constant declaration. Here is a declaration that creates symbolic constants of type CHAR:

```
const
    BLANK =  ' '  ;
    PLUS =  '+'  ;
    MINUS =  '-'  ;
```

The identifiers BLANK, PLUS, and MINUS will now behave as if they were the original characters. It is especially useful to declare a constant of type CHAR when some character has been selected to indicate a specific condition. In program LETTERFREQ, for instance, the character '@' could have been used to indicate the end of the input text. To improve readability, the end-of-text character could have been given a meaningful name. Thus:

```
const
    FINISHED = '@'
        .
        .
        .
READ(TEXT)  ;
while TEXT  < >  FINISHED do
 begin
   if (TEXT > = 'A') and (TEXT < = 'Z')
       then LETTERS[TEXT]  := LETTERS[TEXT]+1 ;
   READ(TEXT)
 end  ;
```

10.2 STRING VARIABLES

A string is a sequence of characters. You have already encountered strings as arguments to WRITE and WRITELN. The following WRITELN statement prints a string on the user's input-output terminal:

WRITELN ('To be or not to be?')

This string contains 19 characters. In programming terms, it is logical to think of this string as an array of characters--in other words, as an array whose component type is CHAR. If you wanted to, you could declare a variable of this type:

```
var
      HAMLET : packed array[1..19] of CHAR
```

The variable HAMLET is a <u>string variable</u>. A string variable is a packed array whose component type is CHAR and whose subscript type has a lower bound of 1. HAMLET can now be assigned a string value, like this:

```
HAMLET :=  'To be or not to be?'
```

Since HAMLET has been declared to have 19 characters, any value assigned to HAMLET must have exactly 19 characters as well. Otherwise, a type mismatch will result. To place a smaller string in HAMLET, one would ordinarily pad the string with trailing blanks so that it will have the proper size:

```
HAMLET := 'Alas, poor York          '
```

The string 'Alas, poor York' is 15 characters long, so 4 blanks were added on its right. The following assignments are also valid:

```
HAMLET := '12345                '
HAMLET := '+-*/                 '
HAMLET := '                     '
HAMLET := 'I think I''m lost     '
```

The fourth assignment demonstrates an exceptional case: namely, the use of quotation marks within strings. Since quotation marks are used to delimit strings, it would be ambiguous to write a string like this:

```
'I think I'm lost    '
```

The computer would not always be able to decide which quotation mark indicates the end of the string. To prevent this ambiguity, Pascal requires that quotation marks within strings be written doubly, as in the assignment above. Inside the computer, the string will be stored in its correct, single-quotation form.
To read a string from the user, one would use the READ and READLN statements. Some versions of Pascal do not allow string variables to appear in READ or READLN statements; others allow you to write statements like

        READ(HAMLET)

    After a string variable has been given a
value, it can be printed with WRITE and WRITELN.
The following statement will print the value
of HAMLET without the enclosing quotation marks:

    WRITELN(HAMLET)

    Because strings are simply arrays whose com-
ponent type is CHAR, they have all the properties
of regular arrays. They can be copied with
a single assignment, and individual characters of
a string can be accessed with array subscripts.
The following loop will print the contents of
HAMLET in reverse order:

```
for COUNT := 19 downto 1 do
    WRITE(HAMLET[COUNT])
```

    Two strings of the same length can be com-
pared with one another using the boolean
comparison operators. The relational ordering
of strings is analogous to the ordering of words
in a dictionary. The leftmost characters are
compared; if they are equal, the comparison
advances to the next character, and so on. Thus,

```
'Tommy' > 'Harry'
'Incorrupt' > 'Incorrect'
'Arizona' < 'Vermont'
'Miscount' < 'Misquote'
'Theme' < 'Third'
'France' = 'France'
```

    A string can also be declared as a symbolic
constant. A string constant is automatically
stored as a packed array. Here are some string
constant declarations:

```
const
    WARNING = 'The time limit has been
                exceeded.' ;
    TITLE = 'Payroll Accounts' ;
    ALPHABET = 'ABCDEFGHIJKLMNOPQRSTUVWXYZ' ;
```

10.3   SOME TYPICAL STRING OPERATIONS

The primitive string manipulations presented in Section 10.2 can be used to form manipulations of greater sophistication. This section will demonstrate a handful of these manipulations with simple programs and program fragments.

Concatenating Strings   To concatenate a pair of strings is to combine them so that they form a single string. Concatenating the string 'XYZ' onto the string 'ABC', for example, would yield the string 'ABCXYZ'. Concatenating the string '456' onto the string '123' would yield the string '123456'.

Pascal does not provide a built-in function for concatenating strings. Using the array properties of strings, however, this operation can be programmed fairly easily. The program shown in Example 10.3 accepts a pair of strings and concatenates them.

EXAMPLE 10.3:   Concatenation

```
program CONCAT(INPUT,OUTPUT)  ;

(*   This program accepts a pair of strings from
     the user and concatenates them.   *)

type
     SHORTSTRING = packed array[1..3] of CHAR  ;
     LONGSTRING = packed array[1..6] of CHAR  ;
var
     STRING1,STRING2  :  SHORTSTRING  ;
     RESULT :  LONGSTRING  ;
     COUNT : INTEGER  ;

begin
(*  -- Read the strings --  *)
     WRITELN(' Please enter the first three character
             string:')  ;
     READ(STRING1)  ;
     WRITELN(' Please enter the second three character
             string:')  ;
     READ(STRING2)  ;

(*  -- Concatenate the strings --  *)
     for COUNT := 1 to 3 do
         RESULT[COUNT] := STRING1[COUNT]  ;
     for COUNT := 4 to 6 do
         RESULT[COUNT] := STRING2[COUNT-3]  ;
     WRITELN(' The concatenated string is ',RESULT)
end.
```

The concatenation sequence in this program is a straightforward one. The first _for_ loop places the contents of STRING1 into the first part of RESULT; the second _for_ loop places the contents of STRING2 into the remainder of RESULT. Although STRING1 and STRING2 have the same length in this example, one could also concatenate a pair of strings with disparate lengths.

Removing Blanks   At times it may be convenient to permit blanks in user input, even if the blanks are extraneous. One way to accomplish this is to read the string from the user and then remove all the blanks at once. Here is a program fragment that removes all the blanks from a string variable named TEXT:

```
NEWPOS := 0  ;
for POS := 1 to TEXTLENGTH do
    if TEXT[POS] <> ' ' then
       begin
          NEWPOS := NEWPOS + 1  ;
          TEXT[NEWPOS] := TEXT[POS]
       end  ;
for POS := NEWPOS+1 to TEXTLENGTH do
    TEXT[POS] := ' '  ;
```

After this program fragment is executed, all the nonblank characters of TEXT are squeezed together into the left-hand side of TEXT. The remainder of TEXT is padded with blanks. The first _for_ loop examines every character to determine whether it is a blank. If it is, then it is moved leftward to the position indicated by NEWPOS. The second _for_ loop adds trailing blanks to the string. Thus, the input string

'A B C D E   '

would be transformed into

'ABCDE   '

The purpose of NEWPOS (i.e., NEW POSition) is to count the number of nonblank characters. Each time a nonblank character is found, NEWPOS is incremented. As a consequence, NEWPOS always points to the end of the "compressed" string. When another character is to be added to the compressed string, it is added at location NEWPOS.

Recognizing Integers   A string containing a series of digits can be converted into the equivalent integer value.   The string '2001', for
instance, can be converted into the integer value
2001.   The program fragment below converts the
string variable NUMBER into an integer and places
the result in an integer variable named VALUE:

```
VALUE := 0  ;
for POS := 1 to LENGTH do
    if NUMBER[POS] <> ' ' then
        VALUE  := 10*VALUE  ORD(NUMBER[POST])
                - ORD('0')  ;
```

Each time a new digit is examined, VALUE is
"shifted" to the left with a multiplication; the
new digit is then added to the one's place of
VALUE.   The if statement is included so that the
loop will not attempt to process trailing blanks.
Here is a slightly more flexible version that
checks for leading plus and minus signs:

```
VALUE := 0  ;
if NUMBER[1] = '-' then
    SIGN := -1
else
    SIGN := 1  ;
if (NUMBER[1] = '-') or (NUMBER[1] = '+') then
    START := 2
else
    START := 1  ;
for POS := START TO LENGTH do
    if NUMBER[POS] <> ' ' then
        VALUE := 10*VALUE + ORD(NUMBER[POS]0 -
                ORD('0')  ;
VALUE := VALUE*SIGN  ;
```

The first if determines whether the multiplier
SIGN should be 1 or -1.   The second if determines
whether START should be adjusted to skip over a
leading sign character. (When the first character
of NUMBER is '+' or '-', START is set equal to 2
so that the for loop will not examine the sign.)

Extracting Substrings   A substring is a fragment
of a larger string.   Given the string 'ABCDEF', a
list of possible substrings might include

```
'ABC'
'BC'
'CDEF'
'E'
```

It is often convenient to specify a substring in terms of two numbers: its starting position in the host string and its length. The string 'ABC', for instance, begins at position #1 of 'ABCDEF' and is three characters long. Here is a loop that will print any substring of NAME given its position and its length:

```
for COUNT := STARTPOS to STARTPOS+LENGTH-1 do
        WRITE(NAME[COUNT])
```

Alternately, you might want to extract the substring representing the first word in a string. To keep things simple, we will assume that all words are separated with blanks. Allowing this simplifying assumption, the following loop will print the first word in the string variable called NAME:

```
COUNT := 1  ;
while NAME[COUNT] <> ' ' do
   begin
      WRITE(NAME[COUNT])  ;
      COUNT := COUNT + 1
   end  ;
```

Notice that this loop fails when a certain case is encountered. If NAME contains only one word, then the while loop will never reach a blank. Thus, COUNT will continue to be incremented until an invalid subscript error occurs. To rectify this problem, we can declare a constant called NAMELENGTH and rewrite the loop this way:

```
for COUNT := 1 to NAMELENGTH do
        if NAME[COUNT] = ' ' then
                goto 999
        else
                WRITE(NAME[COUNT])  ;
999:
```

Now the loop will advance until a blank is found or until the end of the string is reached-- whichever comes first. When a blank is found, the goto will transfer control to statement 999, which is the statement immediately outside the loop. This approach is somewhat less readable, unfortunately, but it does guarantee that the loop will be terminated before an invalid subscript can be referenced.

Problem Set

*1. Write a program that accepts a string containing a mix of uppercase and lowercase letters and then prints the string entirely in uppercase.

 2. Write two programs that will accept a string containing a Roman numeral value between 1 and 10 (that is, between I and X) and print the decimal equivalent. One program should utilize a <u>case</u> statement; the other should evaluate the string character-by-character.

*3. Is it legal to write a string whose value is a reserved word, like 'BEGIN' or 'VAR'?

*4. What is the value of ORD('XYZ')?

 5. A <u>palindrome</u> is a string which, when reversed, remains unchanged. (Punctuation and blanks are excluded from the comparison.) The following strings are examples of palindromes:

```
'OTTO'
'MADAM, I''M ADAM'
'A MAN, A PLAN, A CANAL--PANAMA'
```

Write a program that determines whether a string is a palindrome.

*6. Suppose you are given the following declarations:

```
type
    ADDRESS = packed array[1..30] of CHAR  ;
var
    ADDRESSLIST :array[1..100] of ADDRESS  ;
```

Write a program fragment that locates and prints the "smallest" string in ADDRESSLIST.

11

Defining your own functions

11.1   <u>FUNCTION DECLARATIONS</u>

Pascal provides a large number of predefined functions. These include arithmetic functions, such as ABS and SQRT; type transfer functions, such as TRUNC; and input-output functions, such as EOF. Nonetheless, Pascal may lack some function that you would like to use in a particular program. No language can offer every conceivable feature that a programmer could want, and Pascal is no exception. To let you extend the language with features of your own, Pascal provides a mechanism for declaring functions.

Suppose you wanted to perform exponentiation in a program. Pascal's facilities for exponentiation are limited to the squaring function, SQR. You might have a need, however, for exponentiation involving powers greater than or less than two. What you really want is a function that lets you evaluate expressions like

$$3.24^3$$

$$1.414^{-2}$$

$$17^0$$

You might then decide to declare a function called POWER. This function would take two arguments: an integer value and a real value, such that

$$POWER(3.14,3) = 3.14^3 = 30.9591$$

$$POWER(1.414,-2) = 1.414^{-2} = 0.5$$

$$POWER(17,0) = 17^0 = 1.0$$

Example 11.1 shows a function declaration for POWER. Once declared, POWER can be used just like a predefined function. A function declaration in a program goes between the variable declarations and the program body itself.

The first line of the declaration is the function header. The function header specifies the name of the function, the number and the type of its parameters, and the type of the value returned by the function. A function name is an identifier; as such, it must conform to the requirements imposed upon other identifiers. It must begin with a letter; it must consist entirely of letters and numbers; and it cannot conflict with a reserved word. The following function headers are therefore invalid:

```
function 90DEGREE(ANGLE : REAL) : REAL
function DIGIT?(NEXT : CHAR) : BOOLEAN
function BEGIN(ROW : INTEGER) : CHAR
```

The items listed in the parentheses are the function parameters. POWER has two parameters: FACTOR (of type REAL) and EXPONENT (of type INTEGER). Every time POWER is called, FACTOR and EXPONENT are given the values of the corresponding arguments. Within the function body, FACTOR and EXPONENT can then be used like ordinary variables. Here are some assignments that call POWER:

```
HYPOTENUSE := SQRT(POWER(A,2) + POWER (B,2))
VOLUME := POWER(LENGTH,3)
RANK := 2 + POWER(SCORE/2,TRUNC(OLDRANK))
```

Each argument must have the same type as its corresponding entry in the function header. When an argument is an expression, as in the third assignment above, the result of the expression is calculated before it is passed to the function. Consequently, if SCORE equals 4.0 and OLDRANK equals 3.5, then FACTOR and EXPONENT will be given the values 2.0 and 3 respectively.

EXAMPLE 11.1:   Exponentiation

```
      function POWER(FACTOR : REAL; EXPONENT : INTEGER) :
                  REAL  ;

      (*  This function raises a real number to an integer power. *)

      var
           COUNT : INTEGER  ;
           TEMPFACTOR : REAL  ;

      begin
           if EXPONENT = 0 then
             POWER := 1
           else
             begin
                 TEMPFACTOR := FACTOR  ;
                 for COUNT := 2 to ABS(EXPONENT) do
                     TEMPFACTOR := TEMPFACTOR * FACTOR  ;
                 if EXPONENT < 0 then
                     POWER := 1/TEMPFACTOR
                 else
                     POWER := TEMPFACTOR
             end
      end ;  (* of POWER *)
```

FUNCTION HEADER

General Forms: function name(parameter list) : result type
              function name : result type

The result type is a type identifier that specifies the type of the value returned by the function. The parameter list designates the parameters of the function. If no parameter list is specified, then no arguments can be passed to the function.

Examples:
```
    function ARCTAN(THETA : REAL) : REAL
    function ADDCOLORS(COLOR1,COLOR2 : HUE) :
            HUE
    function TSCORE(DEGREES : INTEGER;
                SIGNIF : REAL) : REAL
    function DEVICEREADY : BOOLEAN
```

The result type of a function can be either an ordinal type or the type REAL; it cannot be an array or any other structured type. Within this constraint, the selection of a result type is a fairly flexible matter: it can be a predefined type, like REAL or BOOLEAN, or it can be a user-declared type. In either case, the result type must be specified with a type identifier. The following headers are invalid because the result types are not specified with type identifiers:

```
function SEASON(THISMONTH : MONTHS) :
        (WINTER,SPRING,SUMMER,FALL)
function DAYSINMONTH(THISMONTH : MONTHS) :
        1..31
```

Selection of a parameter type is even more flexible still: any type, including an array type, may be associated with a parameter. Once again, it is necessary to use type identifiers to specify the types desired. (Remember that type declarations can be used to designate a type identifier for a new data type.)

When several parameters have the same type, you can abbreviate the parameter list by grouping those parameters together. It is especially useful to group a set of parameters when they are logically considered to be a unit. The following function headers, for example, have the same meaning:

```
function AZIMUTH(ANGLE1 : REAL; ANGLE2 : REAL;
        LENGTH1 : INTEGER; LENGTH2 :
        INTEGER) : REAL
function AZIMUTH(ANGLE1,ANGLE2 : REAL;
        LENGTH1,LENGTH2 : INTEGER) :
        REAL
```

Following the header, the next element of a function declaration is its internal declarations. Function POWER has internal declarations for two variables: COUNT and TEMPFACTOR. Variables declared internally are not available to the main program--they are temporary variables to be used only within the function. COUNT is used inside POWER as a loop counter; TEMPFACTOR is used to accumulate the multiplications. After POWER is completed, COUNT and TEMPFACTOR will cease to exist until the next time POWER is called.

The final element of a function declaration is the function body itself. The function body comprises the statements that generate the value returned by the function. Any valid Pascal statement can appear in the body of a function. To indicate the value that the function will return, one writes an assignment statement in which the left-hand part is the function name. For instance, the following assignment inside POWER causes POWER to return the value 1:

        POWER := 1

    In the function body, EXPONENT is tested to determine whether it equals zero. If it does, then POWER returns the value 1, because any number raised to the zeroth power is equal to 1. If EXPONENT is not zero, then the exponentiation is performed using TEMPFACTOR. After TEMPFACTOR has been calculated, it is assigned to POWER and hence returned as a result of the function.
    Function MEAN is an example of a function that takes an array argument. LISTSIZE is presumably a constant that has been given an integer value in the main program. If the type LIST has been declared in the main program to denote an array whose component type is REAL (or INTEGER) and whose subscript type is 1..LISTSIZE, then this function will calculate the mean of the values stored in such an array.

11.2   LOCAL AND NONLOCAL IDENTIFIERS

    A program consisting of a main body and a collection of functions can be considered as a series of concentric blocks. The program shown in Example 11.3 consists of an outer block--the program itself--and an inner block within the program. That inner block, in this case, is a function named UPPER.
    Some identifiers have been declared within UPPER: these include LETTER, ONECHAR, UPPERCASE, and LOWERCASE. Since they have been declared internally, they are available only within the function; in other words, they are available only within their smallest enclosing block. These identifiers are said to be local to UPPER.
    Some identifiers, on the other hand, have been declared in the main program declarations: these include LINELENGTH, LINE, and COUNT. They, too, are available within their enclosing block.

```
EXAMPLE 11.2:   Averaging The Components Of An Array


    function MEAN(SAMPLES : LIST) : REAL ;

    (*  This function computes the average of the
        numbers stored in array SAMPLES.  *)

    var
        COUNT : INTEGER ;
        SUM : REAL ;

    begin
        SUM := 0 ;
        for COUNT := 1 to LISTSIZE do
            SUM := SUM + LIST[COUNT] ;
        MEAN := SUM/LISTSIZE
    end ;    (* of MEAN *)
```

Since that block encompasses the entire program, these identifiers can be used anywhere. They can be referenced, not only in the main program body, but also inside the declaration for UPPER. These identifiers are therefore said to be nonlocal to UPPER.

The distinction between local and nonlocal identifiers is very important. A local variable, for instance, behaves quite differently from a nonlocal variable. A variable that is local to a function is recreated every time the function is called. After the function call is completed, the variable is destroyed. Thus, a local variable is not accessible outside the block in which it is declared.

The rules governing the definition of identifiers across program blocks are called scope rules. The scope of an identifier is simply the region where it is defined. When we ask, "What is the scope of X?" we are actually asking, "In what parts of the program can X be referenced?" As it happens, we have delineated the first of Pascal's scope rules already:

Scope Rule #1

An identifier is defined only inside the block where it has been declared.

Identifiers declared in the main program declarations are said to be global identifiers. LINELENGTH, LINE, and COUNT are examples of glo-

EXAMPLE 11.3   Converting to uppercase

```
program CHANGECASE(INPUT,OUTPUT) ;

(* This program accepts an input string and converts
    all of its lowercase letters into uppercase letters. *)

const
    LINELENGTH = 80 ;

var
    LINE : packed array[1..LINELENGTH] of CHAR ;
    COUNT : INTEGER ;

    function UPPER(ONECHAR : CHAR) : CHAR ;

    (* This function accepts one character.  If it is a
        lowercase letter, then the uppercase equivalent
        is returned.  Otherwise, the function returns
        the original character. *)

    const
        UPPERCASE='ABCDEFGHIJKLMNOPQRSTUVWXYZ' ;
        LOWERCASE='abcdefghijklmnopqrstuvwxyz' ;

    var
        LETTER : INTEGER ;

    begin
        UPPER := ONECHAR ;
        if (ONECHAR > = 'a') and (ONECHAR < = 'z') then
            for LETTER := 1 to 26 do
                if ONECHAR = LOWERCASE[LETTER] then
                    UPPER := UPPERCASE[LETTER]
    end ;   (* of UPPER *)

begin (* main program *)
    WRITELN(' Please enter a string for uppercase
            conversion:') ;
    READ(LINE) ;
    for COUNT := 1 to LINELENGTH do
        LINE[COUNT] := UPPER(LINE[COUNT]) ;
    WRITELN(' The converted string is:') ;
    WRITELN(LINE)
end.
```

BLOCK #1

BLOCK #2

bal identifiers. Since global identifiers are declared in the outermost block, they are available throughout the program. The variable LINE, for instance, could be assigned a value or printed inside the declaration for UPPER.

The skeletal program shown in Example 11.4 includes three functions: ENTRY, SEARCH, and BACK TRACK. We can use this program to apply scope rule #1 in a somewhat more complex setting. First, we note that NAMELENGTH, STATUS, FIELD, and USERNAME are global. Thus, they can be referenced throughout the program.

ONECHAR and COUNT are local to function ENTRY. This function declaration includes an internal function of its own: SEARCH. Identifiers POSITION and INDEX are local to SEARCH. Statements inside SEARCH can also reference ONECHAR, COUNT, and the global identifiers. (The constant NAMELENGTH, for instance, is used as the upper bound of a subrange in the declaration of INDEX.)

FINALPOS, BASE, and TRANSFORM are local to BACKTRACK. As a result, they are not available outside BACKTRACK. A statement inside ENTRY cannot reference them, nor can a statement in the main program body.

Suppose we want to declare the same identifier twice: once inside ENTRY, and once inside BACKTRACK. Can we do it? The answer is "yes". An identifier can be given different declarations in separate blocks. The identifier will actually refer to two separate entities. Inside ENTRY, it will stand for the entity declared there; inside BACKTRACK, it will stand for something else. This gives us our next scope rule.

Scope Rule #2

An identifier can be given different definitions in different blocks.

This is not to say that identifiers should be used duplicatively, only that they can be. Such duplication should be avoided, in fact, because it can be a substantial source of confusion to someone who is reading a program. The task of unraveling a complex program is hardly simplified if an identifier refers to a symbolic constant in one block, say, and to a data type in another.

With this cautionary remark in mind, we can proceed to another question: is it possible to redefine an identifier inside concentric blocks?

EXAMPLE 11.4:   A Program With Several Function Declarations

```
    program ANYNAME(INPUT,OUTPUT) ;

    const
        NAMELENGTH = 20 ;

    var
        STATUS : BOOLEAN ;
        FIELD : INTEGER ;
        USERNAME : packed array[1..NAMELENGTH] of CHAR ;

            function ENTRY(ONECHAR : CHAR) : INTEGER ;

            var
               COUNT : INTEGER ;

                 function SEARCH(POSITION : INTEGER) :  BOOLEAN ;

                 var
                    INDEX : 1..NAMELENGTH ;

                 begin
                   .
                   .
                   .
                 end ;    (* of SEARCH *)

            begin
              .
              .
              .
            end ; (* of ENTRY *)

            function BACKTRACK(FINALPOS : INTEGER) : INTEGER ;

            const
               BASE = 7 ;

            var
               TRANSFORM : packed array [1..NAMELENGTH] of CHAR ;
            begin
               .
               .
               .
            end ;   (* of BACKTRACK *)
    begin  (* main program *)
      .
      .
      .
    end.
```

That is, if COUNT is declared in ENTRY, can we
declare it to mean something else in SEARCH? The
answer, again, is "yes." In this situation, the
identifier would be interpreted according to scope
rule #3.

Scope Rule #3

If a statement references an identifier that
has been declared more than once in concentric blocks, then the identifier will be
interpreted in accordance with its nearest
enclosing declaration.

The program in Example 11.5 declares the
identifier COUNT both in the main program and in
function ISPRIME. In both places, the name COUNT
is given to an integer variable. Nonetheless,
the two variables are distinct. Inside ISPRIME,
the identifier COUNT refers to the locally
declared variable; outside ISPRIME, it refers
to the globally declared variable. If ISPRIME
contained an internal function, that function
could define COUNT on yet another level.
The fourth and final scope rule is simply a
a reiteration of a rule with which we are already
familiar: namely, that all identifiers in a block
must be unique. An identifier can be declared in
separate blocks, and it can be declared in concentric blocks, but it cannot be given multiple
definitions on a single block level. A global
variable cannot have the same name as a function, for instance. Likewise, an enumeration
element cannot also be the name of a symbolic
constant.

Scope Rule #4

On a single block level, no identifier
can be declared more than once.

The third scope rule suggests something
interesting about Pascal's predefined identifiers.
In particular, we see that, with respect to the
scope rules, predefined identifiers are no different from programmer-defined identifiers. Predefined identifiers can be treated as if they
were defined in an imaginary block that surrounds
the program, like this:

EXAMPLE II.5   A program with duplicative variable names

```
program PRIMETABLE(INPUT,OUTPUT)  ;

(* This program prints a list of numbers, indicating
   whether each is prime or non-prime. *)

var
   COUNT : INTEGER ;
   START,FINISH : INTEGER ;

      function ISPRIME(NUMBER : INTEGER) : BOOLEAN ;
      (* This function determines whether a number is
         prime. *)
      var
         COUNT : INTEGER ;
      begin
         ISPRIME := TRUE;
         for COUNT := 2 to NUMBER-1 do
            if (NUMBER mod COUNT) = 0 then
               ISPRIME := FALSE
      end ;   (* of ISPRIME *)

begin
   WRITELN(' What number should the list of primes
           begin with?') ;
   READLN(START) ;
   WRITELN(' What number should the list of primes
           end with?') ;
   READLN(FINISH) ;
   for COUNT := START to FINISH do
         begin
            WRITE(COUNT) ;
            if ISPRIME(COUNT) then
               WRITELN(' is prime.')
            else
               WRITELN(' is not prime.')
         end
end.
```

```
          const
               MAXINT = ...
          type
               INTEGER = -MAXINT..MAXINT ;
               BOOLEAN = (FALSE,TRUE) ;
                         .
                         .
                         .
          function SIN(ANGLE : REAL) : REAL ;
                         .
                         .
                         .
          function ROUND(VALUE : REAL) : INTEGER ;
                         .
                         .
                         .
          function ODD(VALUE : INTEGER) : BOOLEAN ;
                         .
                         .
                         .
        ⎧ program ANYNAME(INPUT,OUTPUT) ;
        ⎪              .
        ⎨              .
        ⎪              .
        ⎩ end.
```

Although this point is primarily of technical
interest, it has a surprising implication: just as
a low-level declaration can redefine a global identifier, it is also possible to redefine a predefined identifier. Needless to say, this is not
a practice to be encouraged.

11.3   BEWARE OF SIDE EFFECTS

When viewed in a rigorous mathematical sense, a
function can have only one effect: to return a
value. In Pascal, however, a function can also
do other things. A function can alter the value
of a global variable, for example, or it can
generate printed output. These additional
processes are called side effects of the function.
Ideally, one would like to treat a function
like a "black box" that accepts a set of arguments
and uses them to create a single result. That is,
one would like to be able to call a function with
the expectation that it will not disturb other
processes in the program. This view of functions
is desirable because it means that the programmer

need have no concern for the internal workings of a function.

Side effects cause a function to behave quite differently. A function with side effects is no longer a "black box" with well-defined inputs and a single, well-isolated result. It is, instead, a far less predictable creature whose design details must be a constant concern of the programmer. For this reason, you should try not to incorporate side effects into the functions you write.

It is possible to create side effects unintentionally. In Example 11.6, ANGLE is the name of a global variable and a local variable. In the main program body, it is used as a loop index; inside DISTANCE, it is used for temporary storage. The program will fail in its present form, however, because the programmer forgot to declare ANGLE inside DISTANCE. Each reference to ANGLE is therefore a reference to the global variable. This means that each call to function DISTANCE will have an unpleasant side effect-- it will alter the value of the loop index.

11.4   RECURSIVE FUNCTIONS

A function can be invoked by any of three callers: the body of the main program, the body of another function, or itself. The first two entries in this list should come as no surprise. The third, however, may be puzzling: why should a function call itself? As it happens, such functions are not uncommon. A function that invokes itself is said to be a recursive function.

Some mathematical functions are most naturally expressed in a recursive form. The factorial of X, written X!, is the product of all the integers between 1 and X. Defined nonrecursively, X! equals X*(X-1)*(X-2)...*3*2*1. Here is a recursive definition:

        for X > 0,   X! = X * (X-1)!
        for X = 0,   X! = 1

The program shown in Example 11.7 uses this algorithm. FACTORIAL is a recursive function that continues to call itself until the condition NUMBER=0 is reached.

Each time a recursive call is made, a new

EXAMPLE 11.6   An unintended side effect

```
program MISTAKE(INPUT,OUTPUT)  ;

(*    This program produces a table showing the distance
      to an object whose height and angle of elevation
      are known.  *)

var
      ANGLE, ALTITUDE: REAL ;

function DISTANCE(ELEVATION,HEIGHT : REAL) : REAL ;
const
      PI = 3.14159 ;
begin
      ANGLE := ELEVATION * (PI/180); (* degrees to
                                radians *)
      DISTANCE := HEIGHT/(SIN(ANGLE)/COS(ANGLE))
end :  (* of DISTANCE *)

begin
      WRITELN(' What is the altitude of the object?')  ;
      READLN(ALTITUDE) ;
      WRITELN(' ') ;
      WRITELN(' Elevation':20,'Distance':10) ;
      ANGLE := 0 ;
      while ANGLE < = 90 do
          begin
                WRITELN(ANGLE:20:3,DISTANCE(ANGLE,
                        ALTITUDE):10:3) ;
                ANGLE := ANGLE + 0.5
          end
end.
```

set of local variables is created. Thus, a recursive call does not affect the variables inside the calling function. If FACTORIAL is initially given the argument 5, here is the calling sequence that will result:

```
FACTORIAL(5) = 5 * FACTORIAL(4)
             = 5 * 4 * FACTORIAL(3)
             = 5 * 4 * 3 * FACTORIAL(2)
             = 5 * 4 * 3 * 2 * FACTORIAL(1)
             = 5 * 4 * 3 * 2 * 1 * FACTORIAL(0)
             = 5 * 4 * 3 * 2 * 1 * 1
             = 120
```

EXAMPLE 11.7   Calculating factorials recursively

```
program FINDFACTORIAL(INPUT,OUTPUT) ;

(*   This program calculates factorials using a recursive
     function.  *)

var
     NUMBER : INTEGER ;     (* input number *)

function FACTORIAL(VALUE : INTEGER) : INTEGER ;
begin
     if VALUE = 0 then
        FACTORIAL := 1
     else
        FACTORIAL := VALUE*FACTORIAL(VALUE-1)
end ;  (* of FACTORIAL *)

begin
     WRITELN(' What is the number whose factorial is to
              be calculated?') ;
     READLN(NUMBER) ;
     if NUMBER < 0 then
        WRITELN(' Negative numbers do not have
                 factorials.')
     else
        WRITELN(' The factorial of ',NUMBER,' is ',
                 FACTORIAL(NUMBER))
end.
```

The exponentiation function is another that can be cast into a recursive form. Example 11.8 shows a recursive version of POWER. Both of these function declarations follow a pattern that is characteristic of recursive functions: they test their arguments for a terminating case. In FACTORIAL, the terminating case is VALUE=0. In POWER, the terminating case is EXPONENT=0. Successive calls in a recursive function should generate arguments that gradually approach the terminating case.

Another class of recursive functions are those involving indirect recursion. Indirect recursion results when a function invokes another function which, in turn, invokes the original function. To prevent the calling sequence from continuing indefinitely, one or both of the functions check for a terminating case. Functions of this sort present a special problem, however: the problem of forward references.

EXAMPLE 11.8   Recursive exponentiation

```
    function POWER(FACTOR : REAL; EXPONENT : INTEGER)
                   : REAL ;
    begin
        if EXPONENT < 0 THEN
          POWER := 1/POWER(FACTOR,ABS(EXPONENT))
        else
          if EXPONENT > 0 then
            POWER := FACTOR  * POWER(FACTOR,
                                       EXPONENT-1)
          else
            POWER := 1
    end ;   (* of POWER *)
```

For technical reasons, a function in a Pascal program cannot invoke another function whose declaration occurs farther forward in the program. If the declaration for function ARCSINE precedes the declaration for function INNERPRODUCT, and if the two are on the same block level, then INNERPRODUCT can call ARCSINE, but ARCSINE cannot call INNERPRODUCT. Example 11.9 shows how the problem arises with indirect recursion.

With any use of indirect recursion, there must obviously be a forward reference. (In this instance, ARCSINE makes a forward reference by calling INNERPRODUCT.) To make indirect recursion possible, Pascal allows us to create an interim declaration that precedes the declaration itself. An interim declaration consists of the function header followed by the word FORWARD. Example 11.10 shows how indirect recursion between ARCSINE and INNERPRODUCT can be performed if INNERPRODUCT is given an interim declaration.

ARCSINE can now call INNERPRODUCT, even though the body of INNERPRODUCT still occurs farther forward in the program. Notice that the parameter list and the function type for INNERPRODUCT appear only in the interim declaration; they are not repeated in the full declaration.

EXAMPLE 11.9   An invalid forward reference

```
        function ARCSINE(SINEVALUE : REAL) : REAL ;
        var
            THETA : REAL ;
            LEG1,LEG2 :    VECTOR ;
        begin
            .
            .
            .
        THETA := INNERPRODUCT(LEG1,LEG2) ;
            .
            .
            .
        end ;  (* of ARCSINE *)

        function INNERPRODUCT(ALPHA,BETA :
                                VECTOR) :  REAL ;
        var
            NUMERATOR : REAL ;
        begin
            .
            .
            .
        NUMERATOR :=  ARCSINE(BETA[2]) ;
            .
            .
        end ; (* of INNERPRODUCT *)
```

Problem Set

*1. Which of the following function headers are
     valid?

```
     function NEXTDAY(TODAY : DAYSOFWEEK) :
                         DAYSOFWEEK ;
     function TAN(ANGLE : REAL) : REAL ;
     function SIGN(CONST : INTEGER) : INTEGER ;
     function MAXINT(INDEX : INTEGER) : INTEGER ;
```

*2. In Example 11.7, which identifiers are local
     to FACTORIAL?

*3. Write a declaration for function ISDIGIT,
     which accepts a single character and returns
     TRUE if the character is a digit or FALSE if
     it is not.

EXAMPLE 11.10   Indirect recursion using interim declarations

```
        function INNERPRODUCT(ALPHA,BETA : VECTOR) :
                            REAL ;  FORWARD ;

        function ARCSINE(SINEVALUE : REAL) : REAL;
        var
           THETA : REAL ;
           LEG1,LEG2 ; VECTOR ;
        begin
           .
           .
           .
        THETA := INNERPRODUCT(LEG1,LEG2) ;
           .
           .
           .
        end ;   (* of ARCSINE *)

        function INNERPRODUCT ;
        var
           NUMERATOR : REAL ;
        begin
           .
           .
           .
           NUMERATOR := ARCSINE(BETA[2]) ;
           .
           .
           .
        end ; (* of INNERPRODUCT *)
```

4. Write a declaration for function PRIME, which accepts an integer and returns TRUE if the integer is prime or FALSE if it is not.

5. If I and J are positive integers, then Ackermann's function can be defined this way:

    ```
    for I=0,     ACK(I,J)  = J+1
    for J=0,     ACK(I,J)  = ACK(I-1,1)
    otherwise,   ACK(I,J)  = ACK(I-1,ACK(J-1))
    ```

    Write a declaration for a recursive function that computes ACK(I,J).

6. Write a declaration for a function that computes factorials without recursion.

12
Defining
your own statements

12.1   PROCEDURE DECLARATIONS

Just as Pascal provides a mechanism for programmer-defined functions, it also permits the programmer to define new procedures. A procedure is a subprogram that performs some specific task. Predefined procedures in Pascal include WRITE, WRITERLN, READ, and READLN. New procedures are declared in much the same way as new functions. Example 12.1 shows a declaration for a programmer-defined procedure.

PRINTBARS is a procedure that accepts an argument of type INTEGER. Notice that the header of a procedure, unlike the header of a function, does not specify a result type. This difference arises because a procedure does not return a formal result; the purpose of a procedure is to perform an action.

Each time PRINTBARS is invoked within the program, a row bars will be printed. The argument passed through BARS will determine the number of bars to be printed. Once PRINTBARS has been declared, it can be used like an ordinary Pascal statement. Here is a for loop

---

EXAMPLE 12.1   A procedure declaration


```
procedure PRINTBARS(BARS : INTEGER) ;
var
     COUNT : INTEGER ;
begin
     for COUNT := 1 to BARS do
         WRITE( '-' )
end ;  (* of PRINTBARS *)
```

---

that uses PRINTBARS to print a triangular pattern:

```
for LENGTH :=  1 to 5 do
     begin
         PRINTBARS(LENGTH) ;
         WRITELN(' ')
     end
```

The WRITELN statement is included to move the output position to the beginning of a new line. The resulting output will look like this:

```
-
--
---
----
-----
```

A procedure can have any number of arguments; each argument can be of any type. Procedures are governed by the same scope rules that apply to functions. The procedure declarations in a program are placed together with the function declarations. For your reference, the accompanying box shows the order of declarations in a program.

Procedures and functions having internal declarations must follow the same pattern as that prescribed for declarations in the main program. In fact, a procedure or a function can be thought of as a program in miniature. They can have their own variables, their own type definitions, and even their own internal functions and procedures.

The procedure in Example 12.2 has an internal function named ISALPHA. The procedure uses ISALPHA to determine whether a character in CHUNK is a letter. If it is, then a dash is

EXAMPLE 12.2   A procedure with an internal function

```
          procedure UNDERLINE(CHUNK : LINE) ;

      var
        POSITION : INTEGER ;

          function ISALPHA(ONECHAR : CHAR) : BOOLEAN ;
          const
            ALPHABET = 'ABCDEFGHIJKLMNOPQRSTUVWXYZ';
          var
            LETTER : INTEGER ;
          begin
            ISALPHA := FALSE ;
            for LETTER := 1 to 26 do
                if ONECHAR = ALPHABET[LETTER] then
                    ISALPHA := TRUE
          end :   (* of ISALPHA *)

      begin
        WRITELN(CHUNK) ;
        for POSITION := 1 to LINELENGTH do
            if ISALPHA(CHUNK[POSITION]) then
              WRITE('-')
      end : (* of UNDERLINE *)
```

BLOCK STRUCTURE

General form:

          header
          label declarations
          constant declarations
          type declarations
          variable declarations
          function and procedure declarations
          body

The elements of a block must appear in this order.
Any element may be omitted except the header and
the body. If no goto statements are used, for
instance, then there is no need for a label declaration section.

printed under it. LINELENGTH is presumably some positive integer constant, and LINE is presumably an array type whose subscript type is 1..LINELENGTH and whose component type is CHAR. Thus, the statement

UNDERLINE('This is a string')

would yield the output

This is a string

12.2   VARIABLE PARAMETERS

At times you may find the use of function calls quite restrictive. Since a function can return only a single value, functions cannot be used in situations where the result is actually a pair of values, say, or an array. By using procedures instead of functions in such situations, you can create a subprogram that returns as many values as you want.

One way to accomplish this is to write a procedure that returns its results by altering global variables. The same effect can be achieved, however, with the use of variable parameters. Example 12.3 shows a procedure that uses a variable parameter to return an array result.

The var preceding STRING in the parameter list indicates that STRING is a variable parameter. A variable parameter differs from an ordinary parameter (that is, a "value parameter") in that all assignments made to a variable parameter are also made to its corresponding argument. If USERNAME were a string variable of type LINE, then the following procedure call would compress the contents of USERNAME:

COMPRESS(USERNAME)

After the procedure call, USERNAME would be modified to reflect the manipulations of STRING

EXAMPLE 12.3   A procedure that compresses strings

```
            procedure COMPRESS(var STRING : LINE) ;

            (* This procedure removes all the blanks from the left-hand
               part of STRING and pushes them to the right. *)

            var
                 POS,NEWPOS : INTEGER ;
            begin
                 NEWPOS := 0 ;
                 for POS := 1 to LINELENGTH do
                     if STRING[POS] <> ' ' then
                         begin
                             NEWPOS := NEWPOS + 1
                             STRING[NEWPOS] := STRING[POS]
                         end ;
                 for POS := NEWPOS+1 to LINELENGTH do
                     STRING[POS] := ' '
            end ;  (* of COMPRESS *)
```

---

inside the procedure. Assuming a value of 10 for LINELENGTH, a possible value for USERNAME might be

'A B C D E '

The procedure call COMPRESS(USERNAME) would change the value of USERNAME to

'ABCDE   '

Since STRING is a variable parameter, the argument corresponding to STRING must be a variable. Obviously, a procedure cannot transmit values through an expression or a constant. For this reason, the following procedure call would be invalid:

COMPRESS('A B C D E ')

When COMPRESS has generated its results, there will be no place to put them unless the argument is a variable. In most versions of Pascal, each procedure and function invocation is checked to ensure that its arguments are compatible with the corresponding parameter

list; if there is a discrepancy, you receive a
warning message. Any combination of value parameters and variable parameters may be specified in
a parameter list. Here are some more procedure
headers in which variable parameters appear:

```
procedure REVERSE(var STRING : LINE;
        var PALINDROME : BOOLEAN)

procedure TRANSPOSE(var GAMMA : MATRIX)

procedure MOVECURSOR(X,Y : INTEGER;
        var SECTOR : INTEGER)
```

In the first example, two variable parameters
are specified: one of type LINE and one of type
BOOLEAN.   The second example is similar to
COMPRESS in that it specifies a single variable
parameter of a programmer-defined array type.
In the third example, two value parameters are
specified, followed by a single variable parameter.
There is one important restriction on the
use of variable parameters in most versions of
Pascal: a component of a packed array cannot be
passed as a variable parameter.   This rule is
admittedly somewhat anomalous. Since a string
is a packed array of CHAR, a single character
of a string cannot be passed as a variable parameter. (In addition, the predefined procedures
READ and READLN use variable parameters. Thus,
they cannot be used to read a value into a single
component of a packed array.)

12.3   PROCEDURAL AND FUNCTIONAL PARAMETERS

As you might expect, a procedural parameter is a
procedure passed as a parameter. Likewise, a
functional parameter is a function passed as a
parameter. Example 12.4 shows a procedure that
takes a functional parameter.

In the parameter list of GRAPH, four parameters are specified: a functional parameter
and three value parameters. Given a function
name, GRAPH plots the function. Throughout the
procedure, FUN refers to the name of the function that was passed. START and FINISH indicate
the range of X-axis values that the graph covers.
STEP indicates the increment that is used to

EXAMPLE 12.4   Graphing a function

```
procedure GRAPH(function FUN : REAL; START,FINISH,
                     STEP : REAL) ;

(*  This procedure will plot a function over any desired
    range of values.  *)

var
   XMOVE,YMOVE : REAL ;
begin
   XMOVE := START ;
   while XMOVE < = FINISH do
       begin
         YMOVE  := FUN(XMOVE) ;
         DRAW(XMOVE,YMOVE) ;
         XMOVE  := XMOVE + STEP
       end
end ;  (* of GRAPH *)
```

---

step the X-axis position. DRAW is a procedure (declared elsewhere by the programmer) that controls the plotting device. Here are some possible invocations of GRAPH:

```
GRAPH(SIN,0,PI/2,0.05)
GRAPH(SQRT,0,100,1)
GRAPH(LN,1,EXP(50),0.5)
```

Notice that the parameter list of FUN is never explicitly declared inside the procedure. It is up to the programmer, then, to make sure that every function or procedure passed as a parameter is compatible with its usage inside the function or procedure where it is referenced. The functional parameter FUN, for instance, is assumed to take a single argument of type REAL.

There is one important restriction on the parameter list of a function or a procedure that is to be passed as a parameter: it must consist only of value parameters. If function F is to be passed as a functional parameter, then the parameter list of F itself may not include any variable, functional, or procedural parameters. As a result, the following functions and procedures could not be passed as parameters:

```
function FINDROOT(function F : REAL) : REAL
procedure INVERT(var DELTA : MATRIX)
procedure WRITELINE(BUFFER : LINE; procedure
                    WRITECHAR)
```

This restriction has a minor corollary: namely, that a function or a procedure cannot pass its own name to itself. Since any function that takes a functional or procedural parameter cannot be used as a parameter in turn, such a function obviously could not pass its own name as an argument for a recursive call. (As it turns out, there is actually no likely situation where such a scheme would be useful in the first place.)

12.4   BENEFITS OF MODULARITY

It is no coincidence that functions and procedures resemble complete programs in miniature. Pascal is designed in such a way that subprograms can be treated as isolated entities whose workings are independent of the main program. As a consequence, functions and procedures allow programs to be designed and constructed in a modular, orderly fashion.

The most apparent advantage of the modularity afforded by subprograms is that it reduces the need for duplicative statement sequences. In nearly every large or medium-sized program, there are at least a few processes that must be performed in different parts of the program. It would be rather absurd, in a program involving trigonometric calculations, to write the formula for arcsines in a dozen different assignment statements. Declaring a function is far simpler.

The utility of subprograms is not merely a matter of convenience, however. Aside from reducing the need for redundant statements, usage of subprograms also allows the various tasks inside a program to be isolated from one another. This isolation of tasks is valuable for several reasons. First, it improves program readability. If the body of a program is cluttered with statements that perform tasks better suited for subordinate functions and procedures, it will be more difficult for a reader to acquire a bird's-eye view of the program. By contrast, a program constructed largely as a collection of well-isolated subprograms can be understood more

readily because its physical structure more
closely resembles its logical structure.

Second, the isolation of tasks within subprograms is an aid to program development.
Programming is, at times, a painful process
owing to the torrents of design details that
arise--particularly in the development of large
and medium-sized programs. Subprograms allow
the programming process to proceed systematically and in manageable increments. They have
the useful effect of permitting a programmer to
consider a program as a collection of smaller
components that can be designed one at a time.

Owing to the nature of program complexity,
this effect is more useful than it may seem at
first glance. As a rule, program complexity
increases <u>geometrically</u> with program size, so
dividing a program into smaller parts actually
reduces the effort required to develop it. Subprograms allow the programmer to minimize
program complexity by adopting a strategy of
"divide and conquer." Starting with a rudiment-
ary statement of purpose for a program, one can
gradually decompose the program into a collection of discrete tasks, which in turn can be
implemented as a collection of functions and
procedures.

As you can see, functions and procedures
are natural complements to the programming techniques that yield considerately written programs.
The isolation of tasks improves program readability, of course, but the story does not end
there. With intelligent selection of function
and procedure names, a program can be made more
readable still. Example 12.5 shows a program in
which this approach has been taken. Each task in
STATS has been isolated to a single subprogram.
Further, each subprogram has been given a meaningful name, so that the main body of STATS can be
understood with only minimal reference to the subprograms. Ideally, the main body of a program
should have a prose-like quality; it should describe <u>what</u> the program does, not <u>how</u> it does
it. The details of the algorithm can then be
relegated to the individual functions and procedures.

EXAMPLE 12.5   A modular statistics program

```
program STATS(INPUT,OUTPUT) ;

const
    MAXSIZE  = 100 ;
type
    LIST : array[1..MAXSIZE] of REAL ;
var
    LISTSIZE  :  INTEGER ;
    LOWER,UPPER : REAL ;
    DATA : LIST  ;

procedure READLIST(var NUMBERS : LIST) ;
var COUNT : INTEGER ;
begin
    WRITELN(' How many items are in your list? ') ;
    READLN(LISTSIZE) ;
    WRITELN(' Please enter the elements of the list: ') ;
    for COUNT := 1 to LISTSIZE do
         READLN(NUMBERS[COUNT])
end ;   (* of READLIST *)

function MEAN(NUMBERS : LIST) : REAL;
var
    SUM : REAL ;
    ELEMENT : INTEGER ;
begin
    SUM := 0 ;
    for ELEMENT := 1 to LISTSIZE do
         SUM := SUM + NUMBERS[ELEMENT] ;
    MEAN := SUM/LISTSIZE
end ;  (* of MEAN *)

function VARIANCE(NUMBERS : LIST) : REAL ;
var
    AVERAGE : REAL ;
    COUNT : INTEGER ;
    SUM : REAL ;
begin
    SUM := 0 ;
    AVERAGE := MEAN(NUMBERS) ;
    for COUNT := 1 to LISTSIZE do
         SUM:=SUM + SQR(NUMBERS[COUNT] - AVERAGE)
                       /LISTSIZE ;
    VARIANCE := SUM
end ;  (* of VARIANCE *)

procedure FINDRANGE(NUMBERS : LIST;
                    var MIN,MAX : REAL) ;
var COUNT : INTEGER ;
```

EXAMPLE 12.5   A modular statistics program (cont'd)

```
      begin
          MIN  :=  NUMBERS[1] ;
          MAX :=  NUMBERS[1] ;
          for COUNT := 2 to LISTSIZE do
              begin
                    if NUMBERS[COUNT] <  MIN then
                      MIN := NUMBERS[COUNT] ;
                    if NUMBERS[COUNT] > MAX then
                      MAX := NUMBERS[COUNT]
              end
      end ;  (* of FINDRANGE *)

      begin  (* main *)
          READLIST(DATA) ;
          WRITELN(' The mean is ',MEAN(DATA)) ;
          WRITELN(' The variance is ',VARIANCE(DATA)) ;
          FINDRANGE(DATA,LOWER,UPPER) ;
          WRITELN(' The range is ',LOWER,' to ',UPPER)
      end.
```

Problem Set

* 1. Write a declaration for procedure SWAP, which
       accepts two arguments of type REAL
       and exchanges their values.

* 2. Write a declaration for function SIGMA.
       Given a function F and an integer i, SIGMA
       should calculate

$$\sum_{j=1}^{i} F(j)$$

       That is, it should find the sum F(1) + F(2)
       + ... + F(i-1) + F(i).

  3. Write a procedure with the following header:

       procedure NUMSTRING(NUMBER : REAL;
                           var STRING : LINE)

       NUMSTRING should convert the value of NUMBER
       into its string equivalent, returning the
       result in STRING. (You may assume that
       LINELENGTH contains the length of LINE.)

Problem Set (cont'd)

Here are some possible values of NUMBER and the expected string conversion:

```
10          '10        '
5.0E-3      '0.005     '
2.0E+4      '20000     '
-35         '-35       '
```

* 4. First, define a data type to represent quadratic polynomials. (A quadratic polynomial is a polynomial in the form $aX^2 + bX + c$.) Next, write a procedure that accepts two <u>linear</u> polynomials and returns their product.

  5. Write a declaration for procedure PRINTPOLY, which accepts a polynomial represented by the data type defined in Problem 4. The procedure should then print the given polynomial.

13

The importance
of reliability

13.1 WHY PROGRAMS FAIL

One often hears derogatory comments directed at
the inability of computers to produce consistently accurate results. There are countless
well-verified tales of computer-generated
utility bills demanding remittances of $0.00
and of computer-generated paychecks offering
seven-figure windfalls. Such errors (especially the former) are obviously a considerable
inconvenience to their victims.

The things that we call "computer errors,"
of course, are usually not a product of computer
malfunction at all. In most computer systems
(excepting those built in the vacuum tube era),
erroneous results are not ordinarily caused by
mechanical failures of the equipment. Most
often, a "computer error" is actually a programming error. Why should this be?

A partial answer may be found with little
difficulty: programs are fallible because the
people who write them are fallible. A program can
contain bugs for much the same reason that a busi-
ness letter, say, can contain misspelled words.
Both are works of writing; both are subject to
human carelessness.

This answer, however, leaves part of the puzzle unresolved: namely, why is the programming process more error-prone than many other processes which, at least on the surface, are equally vulnerable to human fallibility? If a manuscript has been double-checked by a handful of conscientious proofreaders, you can say with some confidence that the manuscript is free of error; a computer program cannot be verified so easily. Bugs may be discovered in a program months or even years after its nominal completion.

It is probably safe to assume that programmers are not mentally deficient in comparison with authors of manuscripts. The difficulty of making programs reliable lies with the myriad interactions that a programmer must consider. Each input value is unpredictable; if it could be predicted, there would be no need to request it. Further, each different input value can cause other variables to take different values, which in turn can cause variations in the flow of control, and so on, ad infinitum.

This observation suggests a plausible corollary: namely, that programs can be developed with reliability as an early design goal. Complex interactions increase the likelihood that a programming error will be made; therefore, efforts to reduce complexity should make errors less likely to arise. If complexity is a major determinant of reliability, then your choice of programming style ought to affect the reliability of your programs. As it turns out, programming style does have an effect on reliability, and it is one that you can exploit with little difficulty.

You can exploit this effect simply by adopting programming habits that yield comprehensible programs. If that sounds familiar, it should be: to our good fortune, the chances of making an error can be minimized with the use of communicative programming techniques. As we have discussed previously, a program written with the aim of clarity in mind will be easier to develop because its design details will be easier to understand. Thus, considerate programmers assist not only the people who read and use their programs, but also themselves as well.

13.2   TESTING

Even if you are very careful in writing a program, you must still face an unfortunate truth: <u>programs</u> <u>hardly</u> <u>ever</u> <u>work</u> <u>the</u> <u>first</u> <u>time</u>.   Some have greater initial success than others, of course, but the axiom remains valid nonetheless. A non-trivial program probably won't work on its maiden voyage.

That may sound like a defeatist attitude. It isn't, though. It is meant only to jar your complacency. If you go through life assuming that your programs work, then you will never find any of the errors that may be lurking in them.

The process of searching for errors in a program is called <u>testing</u>. You can think of program testing as being akin to the "shake-down" that a new submarine gets before it is commissioned. The point of testing is to give your "product"--that is, your program--a rigorous trial before it is put to use. Fortunately, program testing is different from submarine testing in an important respect: program testing is <u>non-destructive</u>, so there is virtually no cost associated with program failure in a testing situation.

To test a program, one must first devise a suitable collection of <u>test</u> <u>cases</u>. A test case is a configuration of input values that can be used to obtain information about the reliability of the program. If a test case causes a program to fail, then we know an error is present. The programmer is in an interesting bind here, because the most desirable test case, oddly enough, is the one most likely to clobber the program. A test case that works is less valuable than a test case that doesn't work, because the latter gives us more information about the program's deficiencies.

The testing of a program should include three different kinds of test cases: <u>normal</u> cases, <u>exceptional</u> cases, and <u>invalid</u> cases. To clarify the meaning of these terms, let's consider a trivial example of test case design. Suppose we have a program that solves a quadratic equation in the form of $aX^2+bX+c = 0$. What values of A, B, and C should we select as test cases?

We should begin with a series of normal cases. They are "normal" in the sense that they represent straightforward examples of valid input

data. If the program cannot handle these cases,
then it must be flawed very seriously. Here are
some normal cases for the quadratic equation
solver:

        A=1, B=2, C=1
        A=3, B=7, C=3
        A=4, B=5, C=0

If we are satisfied with the results of the
normal cases, we can proceed to the exceptional
cases. Exceptional cases help determine whether
the program is able to anticipate tricky input
data. An exceptional case represents input that
poses an unusual twist, even though it is technically valid. The cases below are exceptional;
can you see why?

        A=5, B=4, C=3
        A=0, B=10, C=7
        A=0, B=0, C=0

You will recall that the quadratic formula
is $(-b \pm \sqrt{b^2 - 4AC})/2a$. If these values were
used with this formula, the outcome would not be
pretty. The first set of values would cause the
square root of a negative number to be taken; the
second and third would cause a division-by-zero
error. Yet all three cases are valid inputs.
The first expression, $5X^2+4X+3$, has complex
roots. The second, $10X+7$, is a linear
polynomial with the root X=7/10. The third,
$0X^2+0X+0$, has infinitely many roots.
After the exceptional cases have been examined, we should devise a series of invalid cases.
An invalid case represents input that is entirely
out of bounds. The case A=0, B=0, C=1 is an
invalid case for our hypothetical program; the
corresponding "equation" is 1=0, which of course
is not an equation at all. Invalid cases like
this one must be accounted for, because a progam
is likely to encounter invalid input during its
day-to-day use.

13.3   DEBUGGING

Having identified an error, we are left with the
task of correcting it. Several debugging techniques can be used to diagnose hidden flaws in a

program; the "best" technique is largely a matter
of circumstance. Most programmers begin with an
informal method known as desk checking.

Desk checking is a form of proofreading in
which the programmer pretends to be the computer.
Using a test case that caused the program to
fail, he or she traces through the program listing analytically in hopes of locating the flaw.
Desk checking is usually the method of choice,
because it forces the programmer to develop a
detailed understanding of the program.

Unfortunately, the efficacy of this technique is hindered by the human tendency to "read
between the lines." Programmers reading their
own programs usually see what they want to see,
even if the program listings tell a different
story. Thus, a typographical error (such as a
reference to SQR instread of SQRT) can be over-
looked quite easily. The tendency to read with
a wishful eye is very strong, and it has only one
antidote: patient attention to detail.

If our efforts at desk checking prove fruit-
less, we must turn to a more sophisticated
approach. Although the specific method will vary
from program to program, it almost always involves
some form of traceback reporting. A traceback is
a list showing a history of the flow of control.
To produce a traceback report, one inserts temporary WRITELN statements at strategic points
throughout the program. For instance, if the
program contains a procedure named NEXTLINE,
then the following statement might be placed
in the body of the procedure declaration:

```
WRITELN(' ** NEXTLINE was called.')
```

If NEXTLINE is being called too often (or
not often enough), this traceback will make the
error more apparent. To make the traceback more
informative, it can be designed to show the
history of some selected variables. For instance:

```
WRITELN(' ** In NEXTLINE, COUNT=',COUNT,
        ' and KEY=',KEY)
```

Each time NEXTLINE is called, the current
values of COUNT and KEY will be printed. This
way, we can monitor both the flow of control and
the values of important variables. The resulting
output will allow us to locate peculiar behavior
in the program.

Once the recalcitrant error has been found, we may be tempted to correct it and then move on to something else. It isn't a good idea to work hastily at this point, however, because many error corrections introduce a set of brand new errors. Alternately, an error correction may cure only part of the error, leaving the rest of it intact. To prevent either situation from occurring unnecessarily, it is wise to test the program again after a correction has been made.

13.4   SUBPROGRAMS AND ERROR ISOLATION

Since reliability is closely intertwined with complexity, we might suspect that subprograms can help to maximize reliability. This is indeed the case. Just as functions and procedures allow a program to be developed more systematically, they also allow a program to be tested more systematically.

The key to systematic testing is error isolation. During any stage of the development process, we would like to have at least a skeletal program that is mostly error-free. This way, with each addition to the program, we can isolate new errors to the new section.

To utilize error isolation in the development process, then, it is necessary to view a large program as a series of intermediate programs; each intermediate program implements a progressively increasing fraction of the desired product. In other words, the specifications for a large program should be broken down into a sequence of programs such that each one represents a well-defined subset of the next. As each increment of the sequence is completed, a new round of testing follows. All errors can then be located and corrected before work on the next increment begins.

The "black box" view of subprograms fits nicely into this scheme. If a program is constructed as a collection of subprograms, each performing a single task, then error isolation will be easy to achieve. A subprogram is a natural increment to use in dividing up the development process. Starting with a handful of functions and procedures and a skeletal program body, we can integrate additional subprograms one at a time, testing each one as it is written.

When errors are detected, we will be able to
assume that they lie in either of two places: in
the most recent subprogram, or in the locations
where it is invoked.

14
Sets

14.1   DECLARING SETS

So far we have examined only one of Pascal's structured types: the array. There are several other structured types, however, among which is the set. In mathematics, one speaks of a set as having some collection of members. For example, here is a set composed of the even numbers between 0 and 10:

{0,2,4,6,8,10}

Here is a set composed of the number 73:

{73}

In Pascal, sets work the same way. They are enclosed in rectangular brackets rather than braces, however. Here are the two sets shown above, written Pascal-style:

[0,2,4,6,8,10]
[73]

Like an array, a set variable in Pascal has

a component type. Each member of a set is a value
conforming to the component type. A set whose
component type is the subrange 0..20, for
instance, might have one of the following collections of members:

```
[0,3,10,20]
[4,5,6,7]
[15]
```

Here are some collections of members that
would be invalid for this set:

```
[-1,-2,-3]
[0,10,20,30]
[1.5,1E+06,6.3]
```

The accompanying box shows the specifications necessary to declare a set variable. The
component type of a set, unlike the component
type of an array, must be ordinal. It is not
possible, for example, to create a set whose
members are arrays or real numbers.
Having declared a set variable, we can
assign it a set value. Suppose we have the
following declarations:

```
type
    DAYSOFWEEK = (SUN,MON,TUES,WED,THURS,FRI,
                  SAT)
var
    WEEKDAYS,WEEKEND : set of DAYSOFWEEK
```

We can now write assignments like this:

```
WEEKDAYS := [MON,TUES,WED,THURS,FRI]
WEEKEND := [SAT,SUN]
```

The first of these assignments could be
abbreviated with subrange notation. Thus:

```
WEEKDAYS := [MON..FRI]
```

From time to time we will want to write out
sets that have no members. Such a set is called
an empty set, and it is written in just the way
you would expect:

```
[ ]
```

Pascal provides a mechanism for determining

```
DECLARING A SET VARIABLE

General form:       name : set of component type

The component type must be an ordinal type.

Examples:
    LETTERS : set of 'A'..'Z'
    COLORS : set of HUES
    HOLIDAYS : set of 1..31
    USEDCHARS : set of CHAR
```

whether some value is a member of a set. The mechanism is a boolean operator: in. Given the previous assignments for WEEKDAYS and WEEKEND, the following boolean expressions are true:

```
WED in WEEKDAYS
FRI in WEEKDAYS
SAT in WEEKEND
```

Conversely, the following boolean expressions are false:

```
SAT in WEEKDAYS
SUN in WEEKDAYS
TUES in WEEKEND
```

Suppose that TODAY is a variable of type DAYSOFWEEK. The following if statement will determine whether the present value of TODAY is a member of WEEKDAYS:

```
if TODAY in WEEKDAYS then
   WRITELN(' Today is a weekday.')
else
   WRITELN(' Today is not a weekday.')
```

The in operator can also be mixed with other operators in a boolean expression. For instance:

```
if (TODAY in WEEKDAYS) and (TODAY <> FRI)
     then
   WRITELN(' Today is Monday, Tuesday,
           Wednesday, or Thursday.')
```

```
EXAMPLE 14.1    Printing the members of a set


        procedure PRINTSET(OUTPUTSET : SMALLSET)  ;

        (*  This procedure prints the members of OUTPUTSET.
            The type SMALLSET is assumed to have the component
            type LOWER..UPPER.   *)

        var
            MEMBER : INTEGER  ;
        begin
            for MEMBER := LOWER to UPPER do
                if MEMBER in OUTPUTSET   then
                    WRITELN(MEMBER)
        end ;   (* of PRINTSET *)
```

Example 14.1 shows a procedure that accepts a set as a parameter. LOWER and UPPER are symbolic constants (declared elsewhere by the programmer) whose values specify the upper and lower bounds of a subrange. SMALLSET is a type identifier that is assumed to represent the type set of LOWER..UPPER.

If LOWER is 0, say, and UPPER is 10, then the following invocations of PRINTSET are valid:

```
PRINTSET([5,6,7])
PRINTSET([2])
PRINTSET([1..4])
PRINTSET([ ])
```

If ROOMSIZES is a variable of type SMALLSET, then the following invocation is valid, too:

```
PRINTSET(ROOMSIZES)
```

Sets can often be used to make a complex if statement easier to read. Here are two if statements that test the same condition:

```
if (TEMPERATURE = 0) or (TEMPERATURE =  32)
    or (TEMPERATURE = 212)
        or (TEMPERATURE = 276) then ...

if TEMPERATURE in [0,32,212,276] then ...
```

Although the statements are equivalent, the second is obviously simpler. Set notation can increase readability in other situations as well. To determine whether a CHAR variable named ONECHAR represents a digit, for example, we can write

    if ONECHAR in ['0'..'9'] then ...

You may have noticed that all the set declarations in this section have used either a subrange or an enumerated type as the component type. The reason for this is simple: each version of Pascal imposes some arbitrary limit on the number of members that the component type of a set variable can include. Unfortunately, this number varies widely, with typical values as low as 16 or 64 and as high as 4080. As a result of this restriction, we cannot write declarations like set of INTEGER, for instance, or set of 0..MAXINT. In many versions of Pascal, it is also impossible to write set of CHAR. Thus, the component type of a set is ordinarily either an enumerated type or a subrange of INTEGER or CHAR.

14.2   MANIPULATING SETS

Pascal provides a number of facilities for performing set algebra operations. These operations include set union, set intersection, and set difference. To illustrate each operation, we will presuppose the following declaration:

    type
        COUNTRIES = set of (ENGLAND,FRANCE,
                            GERMANY,SPAIN,ITALY)

The union of two sets is a set combining the members of the two sets. The symbol for set union is a plus sign (+). Thus:

    [ENGLAND,FRANCE] + [ITALY]──────► [ENGLAND,FRANCE,
            ITALY]

    [SPAIN] + [GERMANY]──────► [SPAIN,GERMANY]

    [FRANCE,SPAIN] + [ENGLAND,ITALY]──────► [ENGLAND,
            FRANCE,SPAIN,ITALY]

```
[FRANCE,GERMANY] + [ ]────►[FRANCE,GERMANY]

[FRANCE] + [GERMANY] + [SPAIN]────►[FRANCE,
      GERMANY,SPAIN]

[ITALY] + [ITALY,ENGLAND]────►[ITALY,ENGLAND]

[SPAIN] + [SPAIN]────►[SPAIN]
```

The _intersection_ of two sets is a set com-
posed of the values that are members of both sets.
The symbol for set intersection is an asterisk
(*). Thus:

```
[ENGLAND,FRANCE,GERMANY] * [ENGLAND,GERMANY]
      ────►[ENGLAND,GERMANY]

[ITALY,SPAIN] * [ENGLAND,SPAIN,FRANCE]────►
      [SPAIN]

[ITALY,SPAIN] * [GERMANY]────►[ ]

[FRANCE] * [FRANCE]────►[FRANCE]

[ENGLAND,SPAIN,GERMANY] * [ITALY,SPAIN,
      FRANCE,ENGLAND]────►[SPAIN,ENGLAND]

[ITALY] * [ ]────►[ ]

[ENGLAND..ITALY] * [FRANCE,SPAIN]────►|FRANCE,
      SPAIN]

[ ] * [ ]────►[ ]
```

The _difference_ of two sets is a set containing all the members of the first set, except those
which are also members of the second set. The
symbol for set difference is a minus sign (-).
Thus:

```
[ENGLAND..ITALY] - [FRANCE..SPAIN]────►
      [ENGLAND,ITALY]

[ENGLAND..ITALY) - [ITALY,SPAIN]────►
      [ENGLAND,FRANCE,GERMANY]

[ENGLAND,FRANCE,SPAIN] - [FRANCE]────►
      [ENGLAND,SPAIN]

[ENGLAND,FRANCE,GERMANY] - [FRANCE,SPAIN]────►
      [ENGLAND,GERMANY]
```

[GERMANY..ITALY] - [ENGLAND..SPAIN]———➤
                    [ITALY]

[ENGLAND,FRANCE] - [ ]——➤ [ENGLAND,FRANCE]

[ ] - [ENGLAND..ITALY]——➤ [ ]

[SPAIN] - [SPAIN]——➤[ ]

These three operators can be used to form set expressions. For instance, if we declare MAP1 and MAP2 to be variables of type COUNTRIES, then we can write assignments like

```
MAP1 := [FRANCE]
MAP1 := MAP1 + [GERMANY]
MAP2 := MAP1
MAP1 := MAP1 * (MAP2 + [ITALY])
MAP2 := MAP2 - [SPAIN] - MAP1
```

Example 14.2 shows a program that uses sets to generate prime numbers. The algorithm is a simple one called Eratosthenes' sieve. Beginning with a set composed of all the integers between 2 and MAXPRIME, the program uses a for loop to check each integer. If an integer is a member of the set, then it is printed; all the multiples of that integer are removed from the set.

EXAMPLE 14.2   Eratosthenes' sieve

```
program SIEVE(INPUT,OUTPUT) ;
const
    MAXPRIME = 15 ;
var
    PRIMES : set of 2..MAXPRIME;
    COUNT,MULTIPLE : INTEGER ;
begin
    WRITELN(' Here are the prime numbers less than ',
            MAXPRIME) ;
    PRIMES := 2..MAXPRIME  ;
    for COUNT := 2 to MAXPRIME do
       if COUNT in PRIMES then
          begin
            WRITELN(COUNT) ;
            for MULTIPLE:= 1 to (MAXPRIME div COUNT) do
                PRIMES := PRIMES - [COUNT * MULTIPLE]
          end
    end.
```

The program prints every prime number between 2 and MAXPRIME. (Of course, it would not be difficult to modify the program so that the upper limit would be an input variable rather than a symbolic constant.) Here is how non-prime numbers are cast out of the set variable PRIMES:

Output	PRIMES
	[2..15]
2	[3,5,7,9,11,13,15]
3	[5,7,11,13]
5	[7,11,13]
7	[11,13]
11	[13]
13	[ ]

You may have noticed that, within the nested for loop, the term [COUNT * MULTIPLE] appears. Is this a set intersection operation? No, it is an ordinary multiplication. It is perfectly legal to use an arithmetic expression to specify a member of a set. There is no ambiguity here, because the component type of a set cannot be another set.

14.3   COMPARING SETS

At this point we have one method--the in operator--for testing the contents of a set. Although the in test is very useful, it would often prove cumbersome if it were the only test available. Consider the set variables MAP1 and MAP2 from section 14.2. To determine whether they are equal (that is, whether they have the same members), we would have to write something like this:

```
EQUAL := TRUE ;
for MEMBER := ENGLAND to ITALY do
   if (MEMBER in MAP1) and not (MEMBER in
      MAP2) then
      EQUAL := FALSE
   else
      if not (MEMBER in MAP1) and (MEMBER in
            MAP2) then
         EQUAL := FALSE ;
```

We can improve this a little, but the cumbersome quality remains:

```
EQUAL := TRUE ;
for MEMBER := ENGLAND to ITALY do
    if (MEMBER in MAP1) <> (MEMBER in MAP2)
        then
        EQUAL := FALSE ;
```

Fortunately, loops like these are unnecessary. Pascal allows the boolean relational operators to be used instead. A test for set equality can be written as a straightforward boolean expression:

```
MAP1 = MAP2
```

The symbol for inequality can also be used with sets:

```
MAP1 <>  MAP2
MAP1 - MAP2 <>  [FRANCE]
MAP1 + MAP2 <>  [ENGLAND..ITALY]
```

The boolean operators >= and <= can be used with sets to determine whether one set is a subset or a superset of another. A set is "greater than" another set if it is a superset; a set is "less than" another set if it is a subset. The following boolean expressions are true:

```
[ENGLAND,FRANCE,ITALY] >= [ENGLAND,FRANCE]
[ENGLAND,FRANCE] >= [ENGLAND,FRANCE]
[ENGLAND,FRANCE] >= [ENGLAND]
[ENGLAND..ITALY] >= [ENGLAND,GERMANY,SPAIN,
                               ITALY]
[SPAIN] <= [FRANCE,SPAIN]
[ENGLAND,ITALY] <= [ENGLAND,GERMANY,ITALY]
```

The following boolean expressions are false:

```
[FRANCE,ITALY] >= [ENGLAND]
[FRANCE,ITALY] >= [FRANCE,SPAIN]
[FRANCE,ITALY] <= [ITALY]
[FRANCE,ITALY] <= [GERMANY,ITALY]
[ITALY..ENGLAND] >= [ENGLAND]
```

The last of these expressions bears a little explanation. Since ITALY is greater than ENGLAND, the term [ITALY..ENGLAND] is actually equal to the empty set. This convention applies to all sets specified with subrange notation. The set [10..1], for instance, is also treated as if it were the empty set.

Problem Set

*1. Which of the following declarations are
     invalid?

A) type
     MATRIX = ARRAY[1..10] of BOOLEAN ;
     ONESET = set of MATRIX

B) type
     EUROPE = (ENGLAND,FRANCE,GERMANY,SPAIN,
               ITALY) ;
     ONESET = set of EUROPE ;

   C) type
        DIGITS = '0'..'9' ;
        ONESET = set of DIGITS ;
        MATRIX = packed array[DIGITS] of ONESET;

   D) type
        ONESET = set of REAL ;

   E) type
        ONESET = set of BOOLEAN ;

*2. Which of the following boolean expressions
     arc true?

     A) 2 in [0..10]
     B) [-3..3] > = [0]
     C) [0..5] * [3..7] < > [3,4,5]
     D) [RED,GREEN,BLUE] < = [RED,GREEN,BLUE]
     E) [5] + [2] = [7]
     F) [5+2] = [7]

 3. A number of people have provided information
     on their leisure time activities. You are
     given this information in the form of four
     set variables: SKIERS, SWIMMERS, GOLFERS, and
     BOWLERS. A person's identity is present in a
     set only if he or she pursues the activity in
     question. Write expressions that yield the
     set of people who are

     skiers or swimmers
     golfers and bowlers
     swimmers but not bowlers
     skiers or golfers but not both
     swimmers and golfers but not bowlers or
      skiers

 4. Write a declaration for function VOWELCOUNT,
     which accepts a string argument and returns
     the number of vowels in the string. For
     example, VOWELCOUNT('Hello there') should
     equal 4.

15
Records

RECORD VARIABLES

Often it is natural to think of several items of data as if they were constituents of some greater whole. Given the house number, the street, and the city of a person's residence, it is natural to group this information together and call it an address. Given the day, the month, and the year of a person's birth, it is natural to group this information together and call it a date. In Pascal, these collections of heterogeneous data can be represented with a structured data type: the record.

A record is similar to an array in that both are composed of one or more individual components. While each component of an array must have the same type, however, the components of a record can have differing types. Here is a declaration that creates a record variable:

```
    var
      ADDRESS : record
                  HOUSENUMBER : REAL ;
                  STREETNAME : packed array
                               [1..20] of CHAR ;
                  CITYNAME : packed array[1..20]
                             of CHAR ;
                  STATENAME : packed array[1..2]
                              of CHAR ;
                  ZIPCODE : INTEGER
                end ;
```

Each component of a record is called a <u>field</u>.
In ADDRESS, the field named HOUSENUMBER is itself
a variable of type REAL; the field named STREET-
NAME is a twenty-character string; and so on. To
reference a field inside a record, write the name
of a record variable followed by the name of the
field. The two identifiers are separated with a
period. A statement that assigns HOUSENUMBER the
value 2300 would look like this:

```
    ADDRESS.HOUSENUMBER := 2300
```

The other fields of ADDRESS can be assigned
values in the same way:

```
    ADDRESS.STREETNAME := 'Main Street         '
    ADDRESS.CITYNAME := 'Anytown             '
    ADDRESS.STATENAME := 'NY'
    ADDRESS.ZIPCODE := 12345
```

Notice that the fields STREETNAME and CITYNAME
have the same type. Since the fields can appear
in any order inside the declaration, it is possible
to abbreviate a record declaration having identically typed fields. The declaration of ADDRESS
can be abbreviated as follows:

```
    var
      ADDRESS  : record
                  HOUSENUMBER : REAL ;
                  STREETNAME,CITYNAME : packed
                      array[1..20] of CHAR ;
                  STATENAME : packed array[1..2]
                              of CHAR ;
                  ZIPCODE : INTEGER
                end ;
```

Every field of ADDRESS can be treated just like an ordinary variable. They can be printed, for instance, and used in calculations. In addition, a record can be treated as a single unit. Suppose we have the following declarations:

```
type
  DATE = record
          DAY : 1..31 ;
          MONTH : (JAN,FEB,MAR,APR,MAY,JUN,
                   JUL,AUG,SEP,OCT,NOV,DEC) ;
          YEAR : INTEGER
        end ;
var
  HISBIRTH,MYBIRTH : DATE ;
```

HISBIRTH and MYBIRTH are now variables of type DATE. HISBIRTH.YEAR and MYBIRTH.YEAR are, in turn, variables of type INTEGER. Aside from manipulating the fields of HISBIRTH and MYBIRTH individually, we can also perform operations on the entire record. The following assignment sets HISBIRTH equal to MYBIRTH:

```
HISBIRTH := MYBIRTH
```

This assignment is equivalent to the statement sequence

```
HISBIRTH.DAY := MYBIRTH.DAY ;
HISBIRTH.MONTH := MYBIRTH.MONTH ;
HISBIRTH.YEAR := MYBIRTH.YEAR ;
```

Example 15.1 shows a procedure that accepts a record as a value parameter. Given the date 3 September 1961, this procedure prints it in the abbreviated form 9-3-1961. (Like an array, a record can be used as either a value parameter or a variable parameter.)

Since an array can have any component type, we can construct an array whose components are records. Here is a declaration for such an array:

```
BIRTHDAYS : array[1..PERSONS] of DATES
```

Assuming that DATES has been declared as before, each component of BIRTHDAYS is a record variable. To print the contents of BIRTHDAYS, we might use a loop like this one:

EXAMPLE 15.1   Printing dates

      procedure WRITEDATE(ONEDATE : DATE) ;

      (* This procedure prints dates in the conventional
          month-day-year (MM-DD-YYYY) format. *)

      begin
          WRITE(ORD(ONEDATE.MONTH) + 1) ;
          WRITE (' - ') ;
          WRITE(ONEDATE.DAY:2) ;
          WRITE('-') ;
          WRITE(ONEDAY.YEAR:4)
      end ; (* of WRITEDATE *)

```
    for COUNT := 1 to PERSONS do
        begin
             WRITEDATE(BIRTHDAYS[COUNT])  ;
             WRITELN(' ')
        end  ;
```

To reference a single field of a single record of an array, we must specify the name of the array, the subscript of the desired record, and the name of the desired field.   This state-ment will print field YEAR of BIRTHDAYS[3]:

```
    WRITELN(BIRTHDAYS[3].YEAR)
```

A record, like an array, can have components with any structured or unstructured type. A field can be an array, a set, or even another record. We will consider some examples of the latter case in the following section.

15.2   THE WITH STATEMENT

Here is a declaration for an array variable whose components are records:

```
    type
      STRING = packed array[1..30] of CHAR ;
    var
      PAYROLL : array[1..WORKERS] of
```

```
record
   FIRSTNAME,LASTNAME : STRING ;
   RESIDENCE : record
                  HOUSENUMBER : REAL ;
                  STREETNAME : STRING ;
                  CITYNAME : STRING ;
                  STATENAME : packed array
                     [1..2] of CHAR ;
                  ZIPCODE : INTEGER
               end ;
   PHONE : record
              AREACODE,EXCHANGE : 1..999 ;
              LINE : 1..9999
           end ;
   PAYSCALE : 'A'..'G'
end ;
```

Notice that two of the fields, RESIDENCE and PHONE, are records themselves. How do we reference the fields of these records? How, for example,

---

WITH

General form: with variable name do statement

Within the specified statement (or compound statement), fields of the specified variable can be referenced by their name alone. The prefixing identifiers can therefore be omitted.

Examples:
```
    with PAYROLL[7].RESIDENCE do
        ZIPCODE := 23186

    for EMPLOYEE := 1 to WORKERS do
        with PAYROLL[EMPLOYEE] do
            if PAYSCALE < 'G' then
                PAYSCALE := SUCC(PAYSCALE)
```

can we print the zip code of worker #7? Since
this field is embedded inside two nested records,
we must provide both its own name and that of the
record surrounding it:

```
WRITELN(PAYROLL[7].RESIDENCE.ZIPCODE)
```

Similarly, here is an assignment that updates
the area code of worker #23:

```
PAYROLL[23].PHONE.AREACODE := 804
```

Here is an <u>if</u> statement that examines the
last initial of worker #58:

```
if PAYROLL[58].LASTNAME[1] in ['T'..'Z']
                                    then ...
```

Putting all the right subscripts and field
names together can be a tedious and error-prone
job.   In some programs, where the same field is
referenced over and over, it can also be a
repetitious job. To help alleviate this repetition, Pascal provides the <u>with</u> statement.

The <u>with</u> statement allows frequently accessed
record variables to be written in a more concise
form.   For example, here is a program fragment
that prints the address of worker #14:

```
with PAYROLL|14|.RESIDENCE do
      begin
            WRITELN(HOUSENUMBER,STREETNAME)   ;
            WRITELN(CITYNAME,', ',STATENAME,
                  ZIPCODE)
      end ;
```

Inside the compound statement following the
<u>with</u>, each occurrence of a field name was auto-
matically associated with the record PAYROLL[14]
.RESIDENCE.   Here is a loop that prints the
address of every worker:

```
for EMPLOYEE := 1 to WORKERS do
      with PAYROLL[EMPLOYEE].RESIDENCE do
         begin
            WRITELN(HOUSENUMBER,STREETNAME) ;
            WRITELN(CITYNAME,', ',STATENAME,
                  ZIPCODE)
         end ;
```

Multiple <u>with</u> statements can be nested.

These three statements are equivalent to one another:

```
PAYROLL[EMPLOYEE].RESIDENCE.HOUSENUMBER := 55

with PAYROLL[EMPLOYEE].RESIDENCE do
   HOUSENUMBER := 55

with PAYROLL[EMPLOYEE] do
   with RESIDENCE do
      HOUSENUMBER := 55
```

We cannot, however, nest <u>with</u>s that refer to records of the same type. Otherwise, an ambiguous construction will result. For this reason, the following use of nested <u>with</u>s is invalid:

```
with PAYROLL[5] do
   with PAYROLL[17] do
      PAYSCALE := 'A'
```

Nested <u>with</u>s should be used sparingly. Aside from the fact that they are easily misapplied (as in the example above), nested <u>with</u>s can also have a deleterious effect on readability. Although the <u>with</u> statement is a convenient shortcut, its usefulness should be placed in the proper perspective. The ultimate aim of a considerate programmer is communication, not concision.

15.3   <u>VARIANT RECORDS</u>

An invariant record is one whose structure always remains fixed. (The records declared in sections 15.1 and 15.2 were all invariant records.) Correspondingly, a <u>variant</u> record is a record that can have different structures in different situations.

Suppose you are writing a program to maintain a list of bibliographic references. If you knew that all the entries in the list were book citations, then you might write the following declarations:

```
const
   MAXREFS = ...
```

```
type
     STRING = packed array[1..30] of CHAR ;
     ENTRY = record
               AUTHOR,TITLE,PUBLISHER,CITY :
                                       STRING ;
               YEAR : 1..9999
             end ;
var
     REFLIST : array[1..MAXREFS] of ENTRY ;
```

What if some of the entries were not book citations? What if some of the entries were citations for magazine articles? If we were restricted to using invariant records, we would have to declare separate arrays to accommodate the different kinds of entries. With variant records, however, we can make the structure of each entry conform to its contents. First, we declare a new type which enumerates the different kinds of entries:

```
ENTRYTYPE = (BOOK,MAGAZINE) ;
```

Now we can write a revised declaration for ENTRY itself:

```
ENTRY = record
          AUTHOR,TITLE : STRING ;
          YEAR : 1..9999 ;
          case ENTRYTYPE of
            BOOK : (PUBLISHER,CITY : STRING) ;
            MAGAZINE : (MAGNAME : STRING;
                        VOLUME,ISSUE : INTEGER)
        end ;
```

This declaration can be split into two parts: the _fixed_ part and the _variant_ part. The fields AUTHOR, TITLE, and YEAR make up the fixed part; they behave just as they would in an invariant record. The rest of ENTRY is the variant part; its structure can vary, chameleon-like, between two alternative definitions.

The first line of the variant part resembles a _case_ statement, but with an important difference: the selector is a type identifier. The values of ENTRYTYPE are used as names for the two defini-tions of the record. When a component of REFLIST has the BOOK definition, the following fields can be referenced:

```
AUTHOR
TITLE
YEAR
PUBLISHER
CITY
```

When a component of REFLIST has the MAGAZINE definition, on the other hand, these are the fields that can be referenced:

```
AUTHOR
TITLE
YEAR
MAGNAME
VOLUME
ISSUE
```

At this point, you may be mulling over an obvious question: how does a program keep track of the current definition for each record? In other words, how do we know that REFLIST[3] contains a book, say, while REFLIST[4] contains a magazine? The usual method for keeping these things straight is to add a new field--called a tag field--to each record. Pascal allows the declaration of the tag field to be incorporated in a slightly abbreviated form, like so:

```
ENTRY = record
          AUTHOR,TITLE : STRING ;
          YEAR : 1..9999 ;
          case TAG : ENTRYTYPE of
          BOOK : (PUBLISHER,CITY : STRING);
          MAGAZINE : (MAGNAME : STRING ;
                       VOLUME,ISSUE : INTEGER)
        end ;
```

The field named TAG is now a variable of type ENTRYTYPE. When a record contains a book citation, we can assign TAG the value BOOK; when a record contains a magazine citation, we can assign TAG the value MAGAZINE. Here is a statement sequence that places a book citation in REFLIST[12] :

```
REFLIST[12].TAG := BOOK ;
REFLIST[12].AUTHOR := 'Thomas Hobbes      ' ;
REFLIST[12].TITLE := 'Leviathan          ' ;
REFLIST[12].YEAR := 1651 ;
REFLIST[12].PUBLISHER := 'Andrew Crooke     ' ;
REFLIST[12].CITY := 'London             ' ;
```

To determine the current status of a variant record, you need only examine the value of its tag field. Example 15.2 shows a procedure that accepts a value of type ENTRY and prints it.

What happens if a program attempts to reference a field that doesn't exist in the current definition? Most versions of Pascal do not detect this error. Hence, the operation will be performed, but it will yield nonsensical results. If REFLIST[12] contains a book, then the following statement will produce garbage output:

```
WRITELN(REFLIST[12].VOLUME)
```

The variant part of a record may have any number of definitions. Although enumerated types are preferable for reasons of clarity, any ordinal type identifier may be used to name the definitions of a variant record. Here is a record declaration that uses a subrange of INTEGER for this purpose:

```
type
    ITEMKIND = 1..3 ;
    STOCKITEM = record
                PARTNUMBER : INTEGER ;
                case KIND : ITEMKIND of
                    1 : (LITERS : REAL) ;
                    2 : (GALLONS : REAL) ;
                    3 : (FLUIDOUNCES : REAL)
                end ;
```

It is plain that a field identifier cannot be used twice in the same record declaration. If the same identifier were used for two fields in the same record--even in different definitions of a variant record--then references to that identifier would be ambiguous. Notice, too, that a declaration for a variant record has only one closing end. Since a record can have only one variant part, the end that terminates the record serves to terminate the variant part as well.

```
EXAMPLE 15.2    Printing a variant record

        procedure PRINTREF(CITATION : ENTRY) ;
        begin
            WRITELN(CITATION.AUTHOR) ;
            WRITELN(TIATION.TITLE) ;
            WRITELN(CITATION.YEAR) ;
            if CITATION.TAG = BOOK then
                WRITELN(CITATION.PUBLISHER,', ',CITATION.
                    CITY)
            else
                begin
                    WRITELN(CITATION.MAGNAME) ;
                    WRITELN(CITATION.VOLUME,' - ',CITATION.
                        ISSUE)
                end
        end ;  (* of PRINTREF *)
```

Problem Set

*1. Consider the following declarations:

```
const
      STRINGLENGTH = 80 ;
type
      STRING = packed array[1..STRINGLENGTH]
                             of CHAR ;
      DATE = record
                  DAY : 1..31 ;
                  MONTH : 1..12 ;
                  YEAR : 1..9999
              end ;
      REMINDER = record
                     MESSAGE : array[1..5] of
                                  STRING ;
                     EVENT : DATE
                 end ;
var
      TODAY : DATE ;
      MEMOS : array[1..100] of REMINDER ;
      CALENDAR : array[1..365] of DATE ;
```

What is the type, if any, of

a)   TODAY.YEAR
b)   MEMOS[2]
c)   MEMOS[4].MONTH
d)   CALENDAR[200]
e)   MEMOS[16].MESSAGE[2]
f)   MEMOS[16].MESSAGE[2][1]
g)   CALENDAR[1].DATE
h)   MEMOS[10].EVENT

Problem Set (cont'd)

2. Write a declaration for a variant record type named FIGURE. If a variable of type FIGURE contains a circle, then it should store the radius; if it contains a rectangle, then it should store the lengths of the sides; if it contains a triangle, then it should store one angle and the lengths of the two sides adjacent to the angle.

   a) Write a procedure that requests a value of type FIGURE from the user.
   b) Write a function that accepts a value of type FIGURE and returns its area.
   c) Write a function that accepts a value of type FIGURE and returns its perimeter.
   d) Write a boolean function that accepts two values of type FIGURE and determines whether the first figure will fit inside the second.

*3. Which of the following combinations are possible?

   a) arrays of records
   b) arrays of arrays of records
   c) records of arrays
   d) arrays of sets
   e) records of sets
   f) sets of records
   g) sets of arrays
   h) arrays of records of sets

4. Write a declaration for a record type that represents accounts receivable information. For each customer, the information should include a list of invoice numbers, the unpaid balance of each invoice, and the date of each invoice. (Assume a maximum of ten invoices per customer.)

   Next, write a program that accepts this receivables information from the user. The program should then identify the customer with the oldest outstanding invoice.

16
Files

<u>SERIAL FILES</u>

Pascal's structured types can be combined to create a tremendous variety of data structures. At this point, however, we are faced with an unfortunate programming limitation: namely, that a variable cannot be preserved after its program stops running. The data types we have examined so far do not allow values to be stored for later use.

Yet a mechanism for storing values on a long-term basis is clearly desirable. For many applications, it is essential. If we are to write useful programs for such tasks as payroll processing or mailing list maintenance, it would be impractical to reenter every item of information manually every time the programs are run. Pascal provides another structured type, the <u>file</u>, so that values can be preserved and then retrieved.

Example 16.1 demonstrates the sequence that is required to store values on a file. First, the name of the file is included in the program header. Second, the file is declared in the variable declarations. Third, the REWRITE state-

DECLARING A FILE VARIABLE

General form:
          name : file of component type

The component type may be any type of the programmer's choice.

Examples:
          WEEKLYSALES : file of REAL ;

          CLASSNAMES : file of
                            record
                               FIRST,LAST : packed array
                                                  [1..20] of CHAR ;
                               GRADE : INTEGER
                            end ;

EXAMPLE 16.1   Writing values to a file

```
program STORENUMBERS(INPUT,OUTPUT,DUMMYFILE) ;
var
      NEXTNUMBER,FILESIZE,COUNT : INTEGER ;
      DUMMYFILE : file of INTEGER ;
begin
      WRITELN(' How many values do you want to store? ') ;
      READLN(FILESIZE) ;
      REWRITE(DUMMYFILE) ;   (* clear the file *)
      for COUNT := 1 to FILESIZE do
            begin
                  READLN(NEXTNUMBER) ;
                  WRITE(DUMMYFILE,NEXTNUMBER)
                        (* store the value *)
            end
end.
```

ment is used to clear the file and prepare it for writing. Finally, the WRITE statement is used to store values on the file.

Example 16.2 demonstrates the sequence that is required to retrieve values from a file. Once again, the name of the file appears in the program header and the variable declarations. The RESET statement then prepares the file for reading. Finally, the READ statement is used to retrieve values from the file in the order in which they were stored.

The WRITE and READ statements used here are somewhat different from those used for terminal input and output. Notice that the usual parameter list is preceded by the name of the file being accessed. The REWRITE and RESET statements also take a file name as a parameter. The following sequence illustrates the effects of these four statements on a file whose component type is INTEGER:

```
REWRITE(DUMMYFILE)            ↑____

WRITE(DUMMYFILE,2*6)          12  ↑

WRITE(DUMMYFILE,3+4,
      4+5)                    12    7    9  ↑

WRITE(DUMMYFILE,20)           12    7    9    20  ↑

RESET(DUMMYFILE)              ↑12   7    9    20

READ(DUMMYFILE,
     LASTNUMBER)              12   ↑7    9    20

READ(DUMMYFILE,I,J)          12    7    9   ↑20
```

EXAMPLE 16.2   Reading values from a file

```
program GETNUMBERS(INPUT,OUTPUT,DUMMYFILE) ;
var
     LASTNUMBER : INTEGER ;
     DUMMYFILE : file of INTEGER ;
begin
     RESET(DUMMYFILE) ;
     while not EOF(DUMMYFILE) do
          begin
               READ(DUMMYFILE,LASTNUMBER) ;
               WRITELN(LASTNUMBER)
          end
end.
```

The up-arrow represents an imaginary marker that moves about inside the file. After each READ or WRITE, the marker advances. After each RESET or REWRITE, the marker returns to the beginning of the file. The sequence above will cause LAST-NUMBER, I, and J to take the values 12, 7, and 9 respectively. To retrieve a value in the middle of this file, one must first read all the values preceding it serially. A file whose components must be accessed serially is called a serial file (All files in standard Pascal are serial files.)

The EOF (end-of-file) function can be used to determine whether the marker has reached the end of a file. If there are more values that can be read, EOF will be false. When the marker is located at the end of the file, on the other hand, EOF will be true. Thus, it is illegal to perform a READ operation on a file when the EOF condition for that file is true.

Example 16.3 shows a program that copies information from one file to another. When the REWRITE statement is executed, the previous contents of RECEIVING are destroyed. (A RESET statement, in contrast, does not disturb the contents of the file to which it is applied.) Any number of file variables may be used in a Pascal program. The files in a program can, moreover, have different component types and different sizes.

16.2   FILE BUFFERS

When a file variable is declared, another variable is created as well. This variable is called the buffer of the file, and it has the same type as the components of the file. Suppose we have the following declarations:

```
type
  AUTO = record
           MAKE,MODEL : packed array[1..10]
                          of CHAR ;
           YEAR : 1..9999 ;
           LICENSE : packed array[1..6]
                          of CHAR
         end ;
  FILETYPE = file of AUTO ;
var
  VEHICLES : FILETYPE ;
```

EXAMPLE 16.3   Copying a file


```
program COPYFILE(INPUT,OUTPUT,SENDING,RECEIVING) ;

(*    This program copies the contents of file SENDING into
      file RECEIVING.   *)

type
    ORDER = record
                   CUSTOMER : INTEGER ;
                   PARTNUMBER : INTEGER ;
                   QUANTITY : INTEGER
               end ;
var
    COMPONENT : ORDER ;
    SENDING,RECEIVING  : file of ORDER ;
    FILESIZE : INTEGER ;

begin
    FILESIZE := 0 ;
    RESET(SENDING) ;
    REWRITE(RECEIVING) ;
    while not EOF(SENDING) do
        begin
            READ(SENDING,COMPONENT) ;
            WRITE(RECEIVING,COMPONENT) ;
            FILESIZE := FILESIZE + 1
        end ;
    WRITELN(FILESIZE,' orders were copied.')
end.
```

Our new file is, of course, represented by the identifier VEHICLES. The buffer of VEHICLES has the name VEHICLES ↑. Every file has its own buffer, which is provided automatically. The name of the buffer is simply the name of the file with an up-arrow attached to it. Thus, VEHICLES↑ is a variable of type AUTO.

Although a file identifier cannot be used in an assignment, a file buffer identifier can be used like an ordinary variable: it can be printed, used in calculations, and assigned values. In addition, a file buffer can be used as temporary storage for values on their way into and out of the file. For this reason, file buffers are generally used in conjunction with the GET and PUT statements. As a substitute for the READ statement, we can use the GET statement to retrieve a component:

```
┌──────────────────────────────────────────────────────────────┐
│  GET and PUT                                                   │
│                                                                │
│  General forms:        GET(filename)                           │
│                        PUT(filename)                           │
│                                                                │
│  GET retrieves the next component of the file and places       │
│  it in the buffer.  PUT writes the current value of the        │
│  buffer onto the file.                                         │
│                                                                │
│  Examples:             GET(DUMMYFILE)                          │
│                        PUT(DUMMYFILE)                          │
│                                                                │
└──────────────────────────────────────────────────────────────┘
```

```
        GET(VEHICLES)
```

After this GET statement is executed, VEHICLES↑ will contain the component of the file following the current position of the marker. The position of the marker will then be advanced, as with a READ operation. Example 16.4 shows a function that uses GET to examine the components of a file.

Each time GET is invoked, the buffer is assigned the value of the next item in the file. A GET statement can be used anywhere that a READ statement can be used. By the same token, GET is subject to the same restrictions as READ. Neither can be used unless a RESET has been performed and the EOF condition is false.

The PUT statement is similar to the WRITE statement. Instead of storing the value of an expression, however, PUT stores the value of the file buffer. As it turns out, the statement

```
    WRITE(VEHICLES,MYCAR)
```

is equivalent to the sequence

```
    VEHICLES↑   := MYCAR ;
    PUT(VEHICLES) ;
```

Notice that, in Example 16.4, function FINDIT has a file parameter. When FINDIT is called, any file variable of type FILETYPE can be passed. Any function or procedure can have a file parameter, as long as it is a variable parameter. (A file cannot be a value parameter.) When using a func-

```
EXAMPLE 16.4    Searching a file

        function FINDIT(var RECORDINGS : FILETYPE;
                    MATCH : AUTO) : BOOLEAN ;

    (*  This function determines whether MATCH is a component
        of the specified file.  *)

    var
        FOUND : BOOLEAN ;    (* Has MATCH been located? *)

    begin
        RESET(RECORDINGS) ;
        FOUND := FALSE ;
        while (not EOF(RECORDINGS)) and (not FOUND) do
            begin
                GET(RECORDINGS) ;
                if RECORDINGS↑ = MATCH then
                    FOUND := TRUE
            end ;
        FINDIT := FOUND
    end  ;      (* of FINDIT *)
```

tion or procedure that takes a file parameter, one must be careful of the file marker. Function FINDIT leaves the marker in the middle or the end of the file; consequently, the programmer must remember to call RESET or REWRITE following each invocation of FINDIT.

16.3   TEXT FILES

To facilitate the processing of files containing textual information, Pascal provides a predefined data type called TEXT. Like the identifiers BOOLEAN, CHAR, INTEGER, and REAL, the type identifier TEXT can be used without any declaration. TEXT can be considered to have the following "invisible" declaration:

```
type
     TEXT = file of CHAR
```

A variable of type TEXT can be processed like any other file variable. The function shown in Example 16.5 counts the number of punctuation characters in a text file.

The file-handling procedures READ and WRITE behave somewhat differently when used with text files. Ordinarily, READ and WRITE can be used only to retrieve and store values having the file's component type. Under this definition, it would not be possible to access more than one character of a text file at a time. READ and WRITE operations performed on a text file are therefore extended to permit values with other types to be retrieved and stored.

When used with text files, READ can retrieve values of type CHAR, INTEGER, and REAL. The WRITE statement can store packed arrays of CHAR as well. Both procedures automatically convert between the character representation of a text file and the internal representation of the computer. (Recall from Chapter 12, however, that a single component of a packed array cannot be passed to READ or WRITE.)

A text file can be divided into strings of characters. Each string of a text file is called a _line_. When a line is stored in a file, it is terminated with a special character that indicates the location of the line boundary. To store a line in a file, one uses the WRITELN statement. Here is a statement sequence that stores three lines in a text file called REPORT:

```
REWRITE(REPORT) ;
WRITELN(REPORT,'The product of two and three
           is',2*3)  ;
WRITELN(REPORT,SQRT(2)/2)  ;
WRITELN(REPORT,'The quick brown fox jumped
           over the lazy dog.')  ;
```

Each of the three statements causes a single line to be written on the file. The arithmetic expressions are evaluated and their results are converted into character form. After these statements are executed, REPORT will have the following contents:

EXAMPLE 16.5   Counting punctuation

```
function PUNCTUATION(var CHARFILE : TEXT) : INTEGER  ;
var
    COUNTPUN : INTEGER  ;
begin
    COUNTPUN := 0  ;
    RESET(CHARFILE)  ;
    while not EOF(CHARFILE) do
        begin
          GET(CHARFILE)  ;
          if CHARFILE↑ in ['.',',',';',':','!','?','''','-'] then
              COUNTPUN := COUNTPUN + 1
        end  ;
    PUNCTUATION := COUNTPUN
end  ;   (*  of PUNCTUATION  *)
```

```
'The product of two and three is      6'
'7.07106E-01'
'The quick brown fox jumped over the lazy
  dog.'
```

If no file name is specified, then the lines
will go to the user's input-output terminal, as
usual. (This is also the case with WRITE.) To
retrieve a line from a text file, one uses the
READLN statement. Here is a statement sequence
that prints out the contents of REPORT:

```
RESET(REPORT)   ;
while not EOF(REPORT) do
    begin
          READLN(REPORT,ONELINE)   ;
          WRITELN(ONELINE)
    end   ;
```

After the execution of a READLN statement,
the file marker is advanced to the next line. If
a READ or READLN statement does not begin with a
file name, then the variable values are taken
from the input-output terminal, as usual. There
is no chance of file name being misinterpreted to
mean something else, because an identifier in
Pascal cannot have more than one meaning.
        It may seem odd that WRITE, WRITELN, READ,
and READLN are used both for file handling and
for user input-output. The reason for this lies
in the fact that the user's input-output terminal

is itself considered to be a pair of text files:
one called INPUT and one called OUTPUT. When no
file name is specified for a READ or a READLN,
the default file name is INPUT. When no file
name is specified for a WRITE or a WRITELN, the
default file name is OUTPUT. Thus, the following WRITELN statements are equivalent:

```
WRITELN('This is a line of a text file.')
WRITELN(OUTPUT,'This is a line of a text
            file.')
```

INPUT and OUTPUT are different from other
files, however. Although they must appear in
the program header, they must not appear in the
variable declarations. The RESET and REWRITE
operations cannot be applied to them, either.
(For this reason, a program cannot write data
onto INPUT or read data from OUTPUT.)
The boolean function EOLN (for end-of-line)
can be used to detect a line boundary in a text
file. If the file marker is located at a boundary, EOLN is true; otherwise, it is false. Here
is a statement sequence that reads a single line
from REPORT, character by character:

```
RESET(REPORT)  ;
while not EOLN(REPORT) do
     begin
       GET(REPORT) ;      (*read a character *)
       WRITE(REPORT↑)     (* print it *)
     end  ;
```

EOLN and EOF can be used without file parameters. The default file for EOLN and EOF is
INPUT. Thus, the following if statements are
equivalent:

```
if EOF then ...
if EOF(INPUT) then ...
```

Many input-output terminals allow printouts
to be divided into pages. Pascal provides a
built-in procedure, PAGE, for placing page bound-
aries in a text file. The default parameter for
PAGE is OUTPUT. After the following statement is
executed, all ensuing output will occur on a new
page:

```
PAGE(OUTPUT)
```

16.4   RANDOM FILES

A serial file, as we have discussed, is one in which a component cannot be read until all the components preceding it have been read. A random file, on the other hand, is one in which any component can be accessed directly. The term random does not have its usual implications of disorder here; rather, a random file allows the program to reference a component somewhere in the middle without first having to skip the components at the beginning.

Pascal does not officially include any provisions for random files. Some implementations of Pascal have snuck random files in, though, because they are very useful in many file applications. Unfortunately, the language features that handle random files are not standardized among the implementations that offer them. The arrangement we will examine is fairly typical, but you may find the version of Pascal on your computer to be quite different.

First, we will write a declaration:

```
var
     STUDENTS : file random of GRADERECORD
```

Each component of a random file is associated with an identifying number. Since file components are usually records, this number is called the record number. The first component of a random file is record number 0, the second is record number 1, and so on. To move the file marker to a particular component, all we need to specify is the file name and the record number. Our hypothetical machine will provide a procedure named SEEK for this purpose. To move the marker of STUDENTS to the first component, we would write

```
    SEEK(STUDENTS,0)
```

Having positioned the marker, we can use GET and PUT to read or update the desired component. If ENROLLEE is a variable of type GRADERECORD, we can write the value of ENROLLEE onto the fourth component of STUDENTS with the following statement sequence:

```
    SEEK(STUDENTS,3)  ;
    STUDENTS↑  := ENROLLEE  ;
    PUT(STUDENTS)  ;
```

The program shown in Example 16.6 examines every component of a random file and determines whether it should be updated. Notice that a random file can be updated in place. That is, a component of a random file can be written over immediately after it has been read. Such an operation would not be possible with serial files; there is no way to "backtrack" the marker of a serial file except by sending it all the way back to the first component with RESET.

Suppose we wanted to update only one account in the example. How would we know which component contains the balance, say, in the account of some irate customer? One way to find out would be to search the entire file until a component is found with a matching name field. If we knew the proper record number beforehand, however, we could make much better use of the power offered by random files. To this end, we might give each customer an account number from which the record number can be extracted.

Problem Set

*1. Write a program to count the number of characters and the number of lines in a text file.

2. You are given two files whose component type is INTEGER. The components of the files are sorted in ascending order. Write a program that merges these two files into a third file which is also sorted in ascending order. For example:

File #1	File #2	Result File
1	-2	-2
3	0	0
7	2	1
15	3	2
	4	3
	5	4
	10	5
		7
		10
		15

3. Write a program to read the contents of a text file and print it in a user-specified format. The user should be able to specify the maximum number of characters per line,

EXAMPLE 16.6   Updating a random file

```
program UPDATELIMIT(INPUT,OUTPUT,ACCOUNTS) ;

(*  This program will examine the credit status of all
    the accounts stored in a random file.  If the credit
    history of an account is good, its credit limit will
    be updated.  *)

type
    ACCOUNT = record
                   NAME,STREET,CITY : packed array[1..20]
                                            of CHAR ;
                   STATE : packed array[1..2] of CHAR ;
                   ZIPCODE : INTEGER ;
                   BALANCE : REAL ;
                   CREDITLIMIT : REAL ;
                   RATING   : (GOOD,FAIR,POOR)
              end ;
var
    ACCOUNTS : file random of ACCOUNT ;
    NEWLIMIT    : REAL ;
    RECORDNUM : INTEGER ;

begin
    WRITELN(' What is the new credit limit for accounts') ;
    WRITELN(' with good ratings? ') ;
    READ(NEWLIMIT) ;
    RESET(ACCOUNTS) ;
    WRITELN(' The following customers will have the new
               limit:') ;
    RECORDNUM := 0 ;
    while not EOF(ACCOUNTS) do
        begin
          SEEK(ACCOUNTS,RECORDNUM) ;
          GET(ACCOUNTS) ;
          if ACCOUNTS↑.RATING = GOOD then
            begin
                ACCOUNTS↑.CREDITLIMIT := NEWLIMIT ;
                WRITELN(ACCOUNTS↑.NAME) ; (*print
                                         the name *)
                SEEK(ACCOUNTS,RECORDNUM) ;
                PUT(ACCOUNTS)
            end ;
          RECORDNUM := RECORDNUM + 1
        end
    end
```

the maximum number of lines per page, and the
line spacing (single or double). If a line
in the file is longer than the desired length
of the print line, then it should be printed
with truncation on the right. Each page
should be numbered in the upper right-hand
corner.

*4.   What is the effect of the following loop?

while INPUT↑ < > '?' do
      GET(INPUT) ;

*5.   Which of the following combinations are
      possible?

      a)   files of records
      b)   files of variant records
      c)   files of arrays
      d)   arrays of files
      e)   files of sets
      f)   sets of files

  6. Write a program for handling address lists.
      It should include facilities for adding
      and deleting entries. The user should also
      be able to request a listing of all the
      addresses within a particular range of zip
      codes.

17

Dynamic
data structures

17.1   STACKS AND QUEUES

A static data structure is one that always has the
same number of components. An array is one example of a static data structure; an invariant
record is another. A dynamic data structure, on
the other hand, can grow or shrink while the
program is running. We have already seen two
kinds of dynamic data structures: the variant
record and the set. Other dynamic data structures can be constructed with Pascal's built-in
data types as a foundation. Among these syn-
thetic structures, two of the simplest are the
stack and the queue.

A stack is a sequential arrangement of data
with one entry point, called the top. Only the
item at the top of a stack can be accessed. An
item can be added to the top or deleted from the
top. The stack is often described as a LIFO
structure. The acronym LIFO means "last in--
first out." Since the last item to enter a stack
is always the closest to the top of the stack,
this abbreviation is a convenient way to remember how the stack mechanism operates.

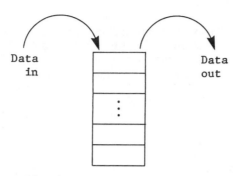

Both in the real world and in programming parlance, a queue is a waiting line. A queue constructed inside computer memory has a real-life counterpart in the queue that might form outside the ticket window of a movie theater: as people at the front of the line are "processed" by the ticket seller, more people are entering the queue from the rear. Similarly, a computer program might alternate between two distinct modes: that of sampling data and appending it to the rear of a queue, and that of processing data at the front of the queue.

Data inside a queue, then, can be accessed at two points. An item can be added to the rear of a queue or deleted from the front of a queue. The first item to enter a queue is always the first item to reach the front. A queue can therefore be described as a FIFO structure, meaning "first in--first-out."

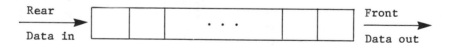

Stacks and queues can be implemented as arrays. A stack whose maximum size is known to be STACKSIZE can be organized as follows:

```
const
      STACKSIZE = ...
type
      STACK = record
                OBJECT : array[1..STACKSIZE]
                               of REAL ;
                TOP : 0..STACKSIZE
                end ;
var
      ONESTACK : STACK ;
```

Each component of ONESTACK.OBJECT is actually a component of the stack itself. Since a stack can grow and contract, a marker is needed to indicate the current size of the stack. Field ONESTACK.TOP performs this function. If ONESTACK is empty, then ONESTACK.TOP equals zero. If ONESTACK contains between 1 and STACKSIZE objects, then ONESTACK.TOP points to the top of the stack within the array.

Example 17.1 shows a procedure that performs a "push" operation; in other words, it adds an object to the top of a stack. The parameter NEWOBJECT is of type REAL because the objects in the stack are of type REAL. (By defining the type STACK differently, we could just as easily manipulate stacks whose objects are of a different type.) Since it is not possible to push an object onto a stack that is already full, the procedure checks for this condition and flags it as an error.

Example 17.2 shows a procedure that performs the inverse of a push operation--namely, a "pop" operation. To pop an object from the stack is to remove it from the top of the stack. Each time POP is called, the top-of-stack marker is decremented so that it points to the new top position. Thus, if all the objects are popped from the stack, the marker will eventually have the value 0, just as it did initially.

When a queue is implemented as an array, it is organized somewhat differently. For one thing, markers must be maintained to keep track of both the front and the rear. A queue whose maximum size is known to be QUEUESIZE can be organized this way:

```
const
      QUEUESIZE = ...
type
      QUEUE = record
              OBJECT : array[0..QUEUESIZE]
                          of REAL ;
              FRONT, REAR : 0..QUEUESIZE
            end ;
var
      ONEQUEUE : QUEUE ;
```

A notable difference between the declarations for STACK and QUEUE is that the array inside QUEUE starts with subscript 0. Thus, the array inside QUEUE contains QUEUESIZE+1 components. Why? The reason lies in the algorithms used to expand queues and shrink them.

EXAMPLE <u>17.1</u>   <u>Adding</u> <u>an</u> <u>object</u> <u>to</u> <u>a</u> <u>stack</u>

```
        procedure PUSH(var NEWSTACK : STACK;
                    NEWOBJECT : REAL)  ;

    (*   This procedure will add the value of NEWOBJECT to
         the top of NEWSTACK.   *)

    begin
        if NEWSTACK.TOP = STACKSIZE then
          WRITELN(' The stack is full.')
        else
          begin
            NEWSTACK.TOP := NEWSTACK.TOP + 1 ;
            NEWSTACK.OBJECT[NEWSTACK.TOP] := NEWOBJECT
          end
    end ;   (* of PUSH *)
```

EXAMPLE <u>17.2</u> <u>Deleting</u> <u>an</u> <u>object</u> <u>from</u> <u>a</u> <u>stack</u>

```
        procedure POP(var OLDSTACK : STACK;
                  var OLDOBJECT :  REAL) ;

    (*   This procedure will remove one object from the top of
         OLDSTACK and place its value in OLDOBJECT.   *)

    begin
        if OLDSTACK.TOP = 0 then
          WRITELN(' The stack is empty.')
        else
          begin
            OLDOBJECT := OLDSTACK.OBJECT[OLDSTACK.
                                        TOP] ;
            OLDSTACK.TOP := OLDSTACK.TOP - 1
          end
    end ;   (*  of POP  *)
```

Example 17.3 shows a procedure that adds an object to the rear of a queue. Since the front and the rear of a queue will continually advance through the array, it is best to treat the array as if it were circular, as shown in Figure 17.1. To make the array wrap around, ADDQ uses the <u>mod</u> operator. If REAR is less than QUEUESIZE-1, then

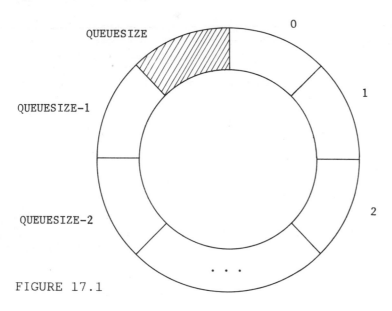

FIGURE 17.1

EXAMPLE 17.3   Adding an object to a queue

```
procedure ADDQ(var NEWQUEUE : QUEUE;
              NEWOBJECT :  REAL) ;

(*   This procedure will append the value of NEWOBJECT
     to the rear of NEWQUEUE.  *)

begin
      with NEWQUEUE do
            begin
                  REAR := (REAR+1) mod QUEUESIZE ;
                  if REAR = FRONT then
                        WRITELN('The queue is full.')
                  else
                        OBJECT[REAR] := NEWOBJECT
            end
end ;  (*  of ADDQ  *)
```

---

it is incremented as usual. Once REAR is equal
to QUEUESIZE-1, however, it is set back to zero.
This is easy to verify: (QUEUESIZE-1) + 1 is
equal to QUEUESIZE, and QUEUESIZE mod QUEUESIZE
always equals zero. (As Figure 17.1 shows,
OBJECT[QUEUESIZE] itself goes unused in this
scheme.)

The procedure shown in Example 17.4 removes an object from the front of a queue. Now we are faced with a puzzling incongruity: why is the "queue empty" state in DELETEQ the same as the "queue full" state in ADDQ? Although the same boolean expression is used in both procedures, different conditions are being tested in each. Because ADDQ increments REAR before the test, it is actually checking to see whether there is more than one free component between FRONT and REAR. If only one free component is available, the queue is considered to be full.

EXAMPLE 17.4   Deleting an object from a queue

```
procedure DELETEQ(var OLDQUEUE : QUEUE;
                  var OLDOBJECT : REAL)  ;

(*  This procedure will remove the object at the front of
    OLDQUEUE and place its value in OLDOBJECT.  *)

begin
    with OLDQUEUE do
        if REAR = FRONT then
            WRITELN(' The queue is empty.')
        else
            begin
                FRONT := (FRONT+1) mod QUEUESIZE ;
                OLDOBJECT := OBJECT[FRONT] ;
            end
end ;  (*  of DELETEQ  *)
```

17.2   POINTER VARIABLES

A pointer variable is one that "points" to another variable. When we say that variable X points to variable Y, we mean that variable X contains the location of variable Y. Here is a declaration for a pointer variable:

```
var
    REALNUM : ↑REAL  ;
```

Inside a program, REALNUM can point to a variable of type REAL. (The up-arrow in the declaration indicates that REALNUM is a pointer.)

To print the contents of the variable that REALNUM references, we say

WRITELN(REALNUM↑)

REALNUM↑ is the real number that REALNUM points to. We can use REALNUM↑ just like any other variable of type REAL. For instance, we can write

REALNUM↑ := SQRT(2)

Where does REALNUM↑ come from? It is not declared alongside REALNUM, nor is it provided automatically. To create a variable for REALNUM to point to, we use the NEW statement. Here is the way NEW would be invoked:

NEW(REALNUM)

When this statement is executed, a new variable of type REAL will be created and its location will be placed in REALNUM. The new variable will have no value initially. Here is a declaration that defines a pair of pointer variables:

var
    I,J : ↑INTEGER ;

At first, I↑ and J↑ do not point anywhere. They can be pictured like this:

I

J

The following statement sequence gives both I and J a location to point to:

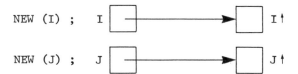

Now we can give I↑ and J↑ values of their own:

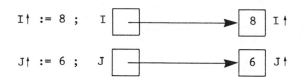

If we next assign I↑ the value of J↑, the result will look like this:

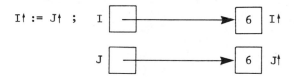

It is also possible to reverse the process. By assigning a pointer variable the value nil, we can return it to its native state. When a pointer contains the value nil, it does not point to anything. (Nil is a reserved word in Pascal.) Here is what happens if J is assigned the value nil:

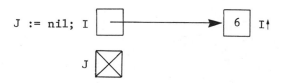

Notice that J↑ is no longer defined. Now let us give I↑ a different value:

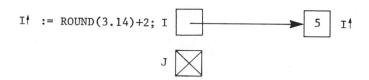

We can set J itself equal to I, with the following result:

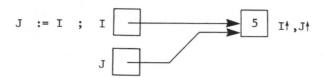

I and J now point to the same location. The location to which J previously pointed still exists; since nothing points to it, however, it cannot be accessed any longer. From these examples you can see that the assignments I := J and I ↑ := J↑ have very different effects. The first modifies a pointer; the second modifies the value of an integer variable.

Assignments made to pointer variables must follow the usual rules of type compatibility. Importantly, a pointer variable cannot be assigned the value of another pointer variable if the two are not declared identically. Since REALNUM is of type ↑REAL, for instance, and I is of type ↑INTEGER, the following assignments would be invalid:

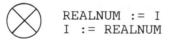
REALNUM := I
I := REALNUM

A pointer that points to a variable of a certain data type is said to be <u>bound</u> to that type. REALNUM is bound to the type REAL; I and J are bound to the type INTEGER. A pointer can be bound to any type, structured or unstructured, as long as it is specified as a type identifier within the declaration. When a pointer is bound to a variant record type, however, the NEW statement can be used in a slightly different way. Suppose we have the following declaration:

```
type
    DOCUMENT = (STATUTE,HEARINGS,BRIEF) ;
    LEGALREFERENCE = record
```

```
                              case SOURCE : DOCUMENT
                                            of
                                 STATUTE : ( ... ) ;
                                 HEARINGS: ( ... ) ;
                                 BRIEF :  ( ... )
                           end ;
              var
                  GERMAINETHING :   ↑LEGALREFERENCE ;
```

To create a location for GERMAINETHING to point to, we can write simply

```
     NEW(GERMAINETHING)
```

This statement will allow us to use any definition of the record. On the other hand, if we know in advance that only one definition is going to be used, we can specify this when NEW is invoked. Knowing that only the STATUTE definition of LEGALREFERENCE will be used, we can write

```
     NEW(GERMAINETHING,STATUTE)
```

Some versions of Pascal include a built-in procedure called DISPOSE. This procedure is essentially the inverse of NEW. NEW creates a new location; DISPOSE destroys an old location so it can be reused. If REALNUM is pointing to some variable, the following statement will destroy it:

```
     DISPOSE(REALNUM)
```

If a variable has been created with the extended form of NEW, then it must be destroyed the same way. Thus:

```
     DISPOSE(GERMAINETHING,STATUTE)
```

Tricks involving pointers and variant records are fairly common in programming litera-

ture, because these two features of Pascal make
some of the internal workings of the computer
accessible to the programmer. As with most
programming tricks, however, the costs of these
maneuvers in terms of readability and complexity
are usually quite large. The purpose of pointers
and variant records is, rather, to help the
programmer create data types in which "form
follows function." In the next two sections, we
will see how pointer variables can be used to
simplify the implementation of some common
structures.

17.3   LINKED LISTS

Suppose you want to keep a list of names in alphabetical order. Names will be added to and deleted
from the list continually. What data structure is
appropriate?

To begin with, you might try an array of
strings. As a new name comes in, it could be
inserted into the array at the proper place. To
make room for a new name, however, the program
might have to move many of the other names forward by one array position:

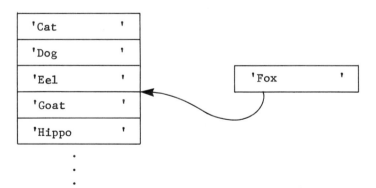

Even if the program left space between names
to facilitate insertion, the array could still
become full in some regions and empty in others.
An alternative representation for the list of
names is a data structure called a linked list.
Here is how a linked list can be pictured:

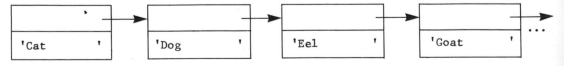

Each item in a linked list is actually a record composed of two fields. The first field contains the data; the second field is a pointer that points to the next item. Here is a declaration for a linked list:

```
type
      STRING = packed array[1..10] of CHAR ;
      NAMELINK =  ↑NAMELIST  ;
      NAMELIST =  record
                        DATA : STRING ;
                        NEXT : NAMELINK
                  end ;
var
      NAMES : NAMELINK ;
```

NAMES points to the base of the list. By following the pointers, we can go through all the names in sequence. (Notice that the declaration for NAMELINK includes a reference to NAMELIST even though NAMELIST had not yet been defined. Pascal allows this exception to the usual rule that an identifier must be defined before it can be referenced.)

Example 17.5 shows a procedure that prints the items (or "nodes") in a linked list. The procedure takes a single argument: a pointer that indicates the beginning of the list. It then follows the successive pointers until it reaches one with the value nil. (A linked list is always terminated by a pointer with the value nil.)

To insert a node into a linked list, all we have to do is modify a few pointers. The nodes themselves do not have to be moved about. Thus:

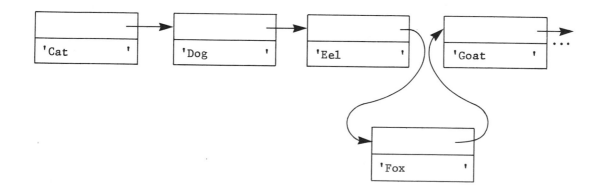

```
EXAMPLE 17.5     Traversing a linked list

        procedure PRINTLIST(BASE : NAMELINK) ;
        begin
            while BASE < > nil do
                begin
                        WRITELN(BASE↑ .DATA)  ;
                        BASE := BASE ↑ .NEXT
                end
        end  ;   (*  of PRINTLIST *)
```

If a pointer variable named EEL points to the node containing 'Eel   ' and FOX points to the node containing 'Fox   ', then the insertion can be performed with the following statement sequence:

```
FOX↑ .NEXT   := EEL ↑ .NEXT  ;
EEL↑ .NEXT   := FOX  ;
```

Now EEL↑ will contain 'Eel   ',

EEL↑.NEXT↑ will contain 'Fox   ', and
EEL↑.NEXT↑.NEXT↑ will contain 'Goat   '.

This algorithm reappears in Example 17.6. Procedure ADDLIST takes a string and inserts it into a linked list. If the list is initially empty, ADDLIST returns a single-node list. Otherwise, the list is searched until the proper position for the string is found. If the procedure reaches the end of the list without finding a string that is lexicographically "greater than" the insertion string, then the insertion string is appended to the end of the list.

Deleting a node from a linked list involves the same sort of manipulation. Suppose NAMELIST points to the node containing 'Cat   '. To delete the node containing 'Dog   ', we would have to modify the pointers like this:

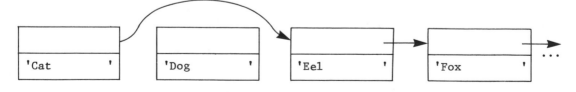

NAMELIST↑.NEXT↑:= NAMELIST↑.NEXT↑.NEXT

EXAMPLE 17.6   Inserting a node into a linked list


```
    procedure ADDLIST(NEWNAME : STRING;
                var BASE : NAMELIST) ;
    var
        NEWNODE,LISTPOS : NAMELIST ;
    begin
        LISTPOS := BASE ;
        NEW(NEWNODE) ;
        NEWNODE↑.DATA :- NEWNAME ;
        if BASE = nil then       (* is the list empty? *)
          begin
            NEWNODE↑.NEXT := nil ;
            BASE := NEWNODE
          end
        else
          begin
            while (LISTPOS↑.DATA < NEWNAME) and (LISTPOS↑.
                NEXT < > nil) do
                LISTPOS := LISTPOS .NEXT ;
            NEWNODE↑.NEXT := LISTPOS .NEXT ;
            LISTPOS ↑ .NEXT := NEWNODE
          end
    end ;  (* of ADDLIST *)
```

Only one statement is necessary to perform
the deletion. The node containing 'Dog   ' is
no longer part of the list, because nothing points
to it anymore. The node containing 'Cat   ' is
now followed by the node containing 'Eel   ';
thus, alphabetical order has been preserved in the
deletion.

17.4   BINARY TREES

In a linked list, each node contains a pointer to
another node. A binary tree is similar to a
linked list, except that each node in a binary
tree contains two pointers. The starting point
of a binary tree is called the root node. A
binary tree is conventionally drawn with the
root node at the top.
The two pointers inside the root node each
point to another tree. One of them points to the
left subtree and one of them points to the right
subtree. In this drawing, root node E points to

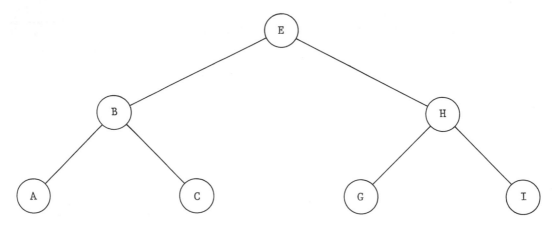

Figure 17.2

B and H. Node B is the root node of the left subtree for E; node H is the root node of the right
subtree for E. Nodes B and H, in turn, point to
subtrees of their own. Except for the nodes on
the bottom, every node in a binary tree has
either one or two subtrees.
     Binary trees have a variety of applications.
In these examples, we will use binary trees to
maintain a collection of strings in alphabetical
order. Each node in our binary trees will contain
a single string. If a left subtree is defined,
its root will contain a lexicographically smaller
string. If a right subtree is defined, it will
contain a lexicographically larger string. A tree
of this particular kind is called a binary search
tree. Here are some examples of binary search
trees:

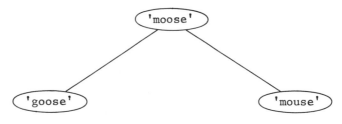

Figure 17.3

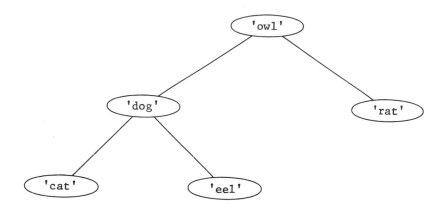

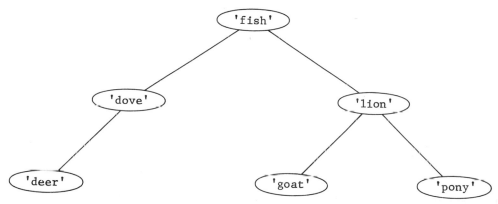

Figure 17.3 (cont'd)

If the type identifier STRING has been defined, we can create a binary tree with the following declarations:

```
type
    TREELINK=  ↑TREE ;
    TREE = record
                DATA : STRING;
                LEFT,RIGHT : TREELINK
           end ;
```

To determine whether a string is contained somewhere in a binary search tree, we can use the properties of binary search trees to simplify the search. Instead of examining every node in the tree, we can start at the root and then follow either the left pointers or the right pointers

depending on the results of a series of lexico-
graphic comparisons. If the node we are examining contains a string that is greater than our
string, we should go left; otherwise, we should
go right. Example 17.7 shows a function that
uses this algorithm.

A similar algorithm can be used to add new
nodes to a search tree. New nodes are always
placed somewhere along the bottom of a tree, so
the tree always grows downwards. Here is an
example of an insertion operation:

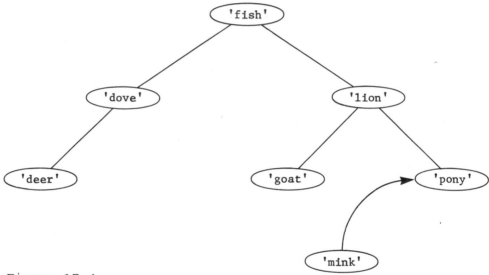

Figure 17.4

Following the tree from its root, we see that
'mink' is greater than 'fish', greater than 'lion',
and less than 'pony'. Hence, the node containing 'mink' becomes the left subtree of the node
containing 'pony'. The function shown in Example
17.8 uses a recursive algorithm to perform this
operation.

To print a binary search tree in its
relational order, we can use a traversal algorithm
called an <u>inorder</u> traversal. The simplest way to
express this algorithm is to define it recursively.
To perform an inorder traversal of a tree with a
given root, a program must complete three steps:
first, it must perform an inorder traversal of
the left subtree; second, it must print the contents of the root node; third, it must perform
an inorder traversal of the right subtree.
When the program encounters a <u>nil</u> pointer,
then obviously the traversal cannot go any
farther along that subtree. Example 17.9 shows

EXAMPLE 17.7   Searching a binary tree

```
        function SEARCHTREE(ROOT : TREELINK; OBJECT : STRING)
                          : BOOLEAN ;

     (*   If the tree contains STRING, then this function will
          return TRUE.  If not, it will return FALSE.  *)

     begin
          SEARCHTREE := FALSE ;
          while ROOT < > nil do
              if ROOT↑.DATA = OBJECT then
                SEARCHTREE := TRUE
              else
                if ROOT↑.DATA > OBJECT then
                  ROOT := ROOT↑.LEFT
                else
                  ROOT := ROOT↑.RIGHT
     END ;   (* of SEARCHTREE *)
```

EXAMPLE 17.8   Adding a node to a binary tree

```
        function ADDTREE(BASE : TREELINK; NEWNODE : STRING) :
                        TREELINK ;
     begin
          if BASE = nil then
              begin
                NEW(BASE) ;
                BASE↑.DATA := NEWNODE ;
                BASE↑.LEFT  := nil  ;
                BASE↑.RIGHT := nil
              end
          else
              if BASE↑.DATA > NEWNODE then
                BASE↑.LEFT := ADDTREE(BASE↑.LEFT,NEWNODE)
              else
                BASE↑.RIGHT:= ADDTREE(BASE↑.RIGHT,NEWNODE);
          ADDTREE := BASE
     end ;   (* of ADDTREE *)
```

EXAMPLE 17.9   Traversing a binary tree

```
        procedure INORDER(BASE : TREELINK) ;
        begin
           if BASE < > nil then
              begin
                 INORDER(BASE↑.LEFT) ;
                 WRITELN(BASE↑.DATA) ;
                 INORDER(BASE↑.RIGHT)
              end
        end ;  (* of INORDER *)
```

---

a recursive procedure that prints a binary search tree using an inorder traversal.

Two other algorithms can be used to traverse a binary tree. In a preorder traversal, the contents of the root node are printed before the two subtrees are traversed. In a postorder traversal, the contents of the root node are printed after the two subtrees are traversed. Unlike the inorder traversal, these two traversal algorithms are not especially useful in conjunction with search trees. For other applications of binary trees, however, the preorder or postorder traversal may be the algorithm of choice.

Stepping back for a moment, you may be surprised to find that Pascal offers only a handful of built-in control structures and data types. In that sense, Pascal is a relatively "sparse" language. Of greater importance, however, is the versatility with which these facilities are endowed. Working with only a few data types, we have been able to design complex data structures and keep them manageably simple. Using Pascal's control structures, we can design programs that are easy to read and easy to use. All in all, Pascal is a good language in which to practice the ideal of considerate programming.

Problem Set

1.   Write a procedure that deletes a node from a linked list.

2.   Write a procedure that reverses the nodes in a linked list.

Problem Set (Cont'd)

3. Design a pointer representation for the queue structure.

    a) Write a procedure that adds an item to the rear of such a queue.

    b) Write a procedure that deletes an item from the front of such a queue.

*4. Write a recursive function that determines whether a string is located in a binary search tree.

5. Write a non-recursive procedure that adds a node to a binary search tree.

*6. Write a boolean function to determine whether two binary trees are equal.

*7. Write a recursive procedure that uses DISPOSE to destroy all the nodes of a binary tree.

8. Design a record structure with fields of your choice. Decide which field will be used to determine the relational order among the different records.

    a) Write a declaration for a binary tree whose nodes contain records of this type.

    b) Write declarations for two procedures: one to insert new nodes and one to print the contents of a particular node.

*9. Write a recursive procedure that performs a postorder traversal of a binary tree.

Appendixes

APPENDIX 1: RESERVED WORDS

and	function	program
array	goto	record
begin	if	repeat
case	in	set
const	label	then
div	mod	to
downto	nil	type
do	not	until
else	of	var
end	or	while
file	packed	with
for	procedure	

APPENDIX 2:   PREDEFINED IDENTIFIERS

Constants: FALSE, TRUE, MAXINT

Types: BOOLEAN, CHAR, INTEGER, REAL, TEXT

File variables: INPUT, OUTPUT

Functions: ABS, ARCTAN, CHR, COS, EOF, EOLN, EXP,
            LN, ODD, ORD, PRED, ROUND, SIN, SQR,
            SQRT, SUCC, TRUNC

Procedures: DISPOSE, GET, NEW, PACK, PAGE, PUT,
             READ, READLN, RESET, REWRITE, UNPACK,
             WRITE, WRITELN

APPENDIX 3: ALTERNATE SYMBOLS

There is some variation among different versions
of Pascal in the selection of typographical
symbols. Although the symbols used in this book
are fairly conventional, some of them are not
universally applicable. Here is a list of the
most common variations:

Typical	Alternate
< =	≤
> =	≥
< >	≠
and	∧
or	∨
not	~
↑	@
[	(.
]	.)
(*	{
*)	}

APPENDIX 4:   CHARACTER CODES

The two most widespread computer character sets
are ASCII (American Standard Code for Information
Interchange) and EBCDIC (Extended Binary Coded
Decimal Interchange Code). The former includes
128 different characters; the latter includes
256 different characters. These character
sets are shown in tables 1 and 2.

These tables show only the printable characters of each character set. To determine the
ordinal number of a character, simply add the
numbers of the row and column in which the character appears. (In ASCII, for instance, the ordinal
number of 'A' is 64+1, or 65.)

The remaining characters are used for special
functions; they have no typographical representation. The most important of these characters are
listed in Table 3.

TABLE 1   The EBCDIC character set

	0	1	2	3	4	5	6	7	8	9	10	11	12	13	14	15
0																
16																
32																
48																
64											¢		<	(	+	|
80	&										!	$	*	)	;	¬
96	-	/										,	%	_	>	?
112											:	#	@	'	=	"
128		a	b	c	d	e	f	g	h	i						
144		j	k	l	m	n	o	p	q	r						
160			s	t	u	v	w	x	y	z						
176																
192		A	B	C	D	E	F	G	H	I						
208		J	K	L	M	N	O	P	Q	R						
224			S	T	U	V	W	X	Y	Z						
240	0	1	2	3	4	5	6	7	8	9						

TABLE 2   The ASCII character set

	0	1	2	3	4	5	6	7	8	9	10	11	12	13	14	15
0																
16																
32		!	"	#	$	%	&	'	(	)	*	+	,	-	.	/
48	0	1	2	3	4	5	6	7	8	9	:	;	<	=	>	?
64	@	A	B	C	D	E	F	G	H	I	J	K	L	M	N	O
80	P	Q	R	S	T	U	V	W	X	Y	Z	[	\	]	↑	_
96		a	b	c	d	e	f	g	h	i	j	k	l	m	n	o
112	p	q	r	s	t	u	v	w	x	y	z	{	|	}	~	

TABLE 3   Special function characters

Function	Ordinal Number (ASCII)	Ordinal Number (EBCDIC)
space	32	64
line feed	10	37
page feed	12	12
bell	7	47
carriage return	13	13

Chapter 2 -- Selected Solutions

1.  ```
    program TRIANGLE(INPUT,OUTPUT) ;
    var
          BASE,HEIGHT : INTEGER ;
    begin
          BASE := 3 ;
          HEIGHT := 5 ;
          WRITELN(' The base of the triangle is ',
          BASE,' cm.') ;
          WRITELN(' The height of the triangle is ',
          HEIGHT,' cm.') ;
          WRITELN(' The area of the triangle is ',
                .5*BASE*HEIGHT) ;
          WRITELN(' centimeters squared.')
    end.
    ```

3.  ```
    A := L*W
    M := R*SQR(R) div SQR(P)
    S := (Y1 - Y2) div (X1 - X2)
    X := ABS(A)
    ```

4. The program contains five errors, any one of which would be sufficient to prevent the program from running:

    a) No semicolon terminates the program statement.

    b) BEGIN is an invalid indentifier, because it is a reserved word.

    c) The reserved word begin should not be followed by a semicolon.

    d) The opening parenthesis in the WRITELN statement is not matched by a closing parenthesis.

    e) The variable TEMP is not declared.

Chapter 3 -- <u>Selected Solutions</u>

1. It is important
    not to confuse WRITE

    with WRITELN. Their effects are
    quite different.

3. program MORESUMS(INPUT,OUTPUT) ;
    var
        ADDEND1,ADDEND2 : INTEGER ;
    begin
        WRITELN(' What are the two numbers that
            you want added?') ;
        READ(ADDEND1,ADDEND2) ;
        WRITELN(' The sum of ',ADDEND1:1,' and ',
            ADDEND2:1) ;
        WRITELN(' is ',(ADDEND1+ADDEND2):1)
    end

Chapter 4 -- <u>Selected Solutions</u>

1.   The fourth and fifth assignments are invalid
    because SIN and COS always return a real
    result. The seventh is invalid because real
    division, not integer division, was used.
    The other assignments are acceptable.

2. 17.693
    17.69
    17.7
    17.7
    1.769E+01
    1.769E+01

3. MARRIED and not MALE
    MALE and not MARRIED
    BLOND and not MARRIED
    not (MALE or MARRIED or EMPLOYED)
    not MARRIED or not EMPLOYED

Chapter 5 -- <u>Selected Solutions</u>

1. The loop will print asterisks endlessly.

2. if X > 0 then
        if LN(X) >= 0 then
            WRITELN(' X to the Y power equals ',
            EXP(Y*LN(X)):1)

```
5.   program TESTPRIME(INPUT,OUTPUT) ;
     var
          NUMBER,COUNT : INTEGER ;
     begin
          WRITELN(' What is the number to be
                  tested? ') ;
          READ(NUMBER) ;
          COUNT := 2 ;
          PRIME := TRUE ;
          while COUNT < NUMBER do
               begin
                    if (NUMBER mod COUNT) <> 0 then
                         PRIME := FALSE ;
                    COUNT := COUNT + 1
               end ;
          if PRIME then
             WRITELN(NUMBER:5,' is prime.')
          else
             WRITELN(NUMBER:5,' is not prime.')
     end.
```

Chapter 7 -- Selected Solutions

1.   Notice that the statement is for...downto,
     not for...to. Since the initial value is
     smaller than the final value, the action is
     not performed at all.

4.   program USEFOR(INPUT,OUTPUT) ;

```
     (*  This program reads a list of numbers and
         their average.  *)

     const
          LISTSIZE = 10 ;
     var
          SUM : REAL ;       (* running total *)
          NUMBER : REAL ;  (* user input *)
          COUNT : INTEGER ;    (* loop index *)

     begin
          SUM := 0 ;
          COUNT := 0 ;
          WRITELN(' Please enter your ',
                  LISTSIZE:3,'-item list.');
          for COUNT := 1 to LISTSIZE do
               begin
                    READ(NUMBER) ;
                    SUM := SUM + NUMBER ;
                    COUNT := COUNT + 1
               end ;
          WRITELN(' The average is ',SUM/COUNT)
     end.
```

5.   Thirty-two times.

Chapter 8 -- <u>Selected Solutions</u>

1. The second and third assignments are invalid
    because they attempt to assign a value to a
    variable with an incompatible type.   (In
    addition, the fourth assignment fails if
    SUNSIGN happens to equal CAPRICORN.)

2. The first declaration is invalid, because the
    lower bound (FRIDAY) is greater than the upper
    bound (MONDAY).

Chapter 9 -- <u>Selected Solutions</u>

1. array[BOOLEAN] of REAL
    array[HUES] of INTEGER
    array[1..10] of 1..10

2. The first has an invalid component type, because
    subranges cannot have the host type REAL.   The
    second has an invalid subscript type.   The third
    and fourth declarations are valid.   Array SALES
    consists of one component: SALES[10,3].

Chapter 10 -- <u>Selected Solutions</u>

1. program CONVERT(INPUT,OUTPUT) ;

```
    (* This program will accept a string and
       convert all of its lowercase letters
       into uppercase letters.    *)

    const
       UPPER = 'ABCDEFGHIJKLMNOPQRSTUVWXYZ'  ;
       LOWER = 'abcdefghijklmnopqrstuvwxyz'   ;
    var
       STRING : packed array[1..80] of CHAR  ;
       COUNT,LETTER : INTEGER  ;

    begin
       WRITELN(' Please enter a string for
                 uppercase conversion.')  ;
       READ(STRING)  ;
       for COUNT := 1 to 80 do
          if (STRING[COUNT] > = 'a') and
          (STRING[COUNT] < = 'z') then
            for LETTER := 1 to 26 do
                if STRING[COUNT] = LOWER[LETTER] then
                    STRING[COUNT] := UPPER[LETTER]  ;
          WRITELN(' The converted string is:')  ;
          WRITELN(STRING)
    end.
```

3. Yes, it is legal. The value of a string has no significance to the computer. The string 'BEGIN' is not treated differently from the string 'IJKLM'.

4. This expression has no value. ORD takes arguments of type CHAR--it does not take string arguments.

6.
```
LOWSTRING := ADDRESSLIST[1] ;
for COUNT := 2 to 100 do
     if ADDRESSLIST[COUNT] < LOWSTRING then
          LOWSTRING := ADDRESSLIST[COUNT] ;
WRITELN(LOWSTRING) ;
```

Chapter 11- Selected Solutions

1. The third is invalid because const is a reserved word. The fourth, although valid, is inadvisable because it defines a new meaning for the predefined identifier MAXINT.

2. VALUE

3.
```
function ISDIGIT(ONECHAR : CHAR) : BOOLEAN ;

begin
     ISDIGIT:= (ONECHAR > = '0') and
               (ONECHAR < = '9')
end ;   (* of ISDIGIT *)
```

Chapter 12 -- Selected Solutions

1.
```
procedure SWAP(var FIRST,SECOND : REAL) ;
var TEMP : REAL ;
begin
     TEMP := FIRST ;
     FIRST := SECOND ;
     SECOND := TEMP
end : (* of SWAP *)
```

2.
```
function SIGMA(function FUN: REAL;
               UPPERBOUND : INTEGER) : REAL ;
var COUNT : INTEGER ;
    SUM : REAL ;
begin
     SUM := 0 ;
     for COUNT := 1 to UPPERBOUND do
        SUM := SUM + FUN(COUNT) ;
     SIGMA := SUM
end ;   (* of SIGMA *)
```

4.
```
type
    COEFF = (A,B,C) ;
    POLYNOMIAL = array[COEFF] of INTEGER ;
```

```
    procedure QUADMULTIPLY(FIRST,SECOND:
                            POLYNOMIAL;
                            var RESULT:POLYNOMIAL);
    var INDEX : COEFF ;
    begin
        for INDEX := A to C do
            RESULT[INDEX] := 0 ;
        if (FIRST[A] < > 0) or (SECOND[A] < > 0) then
            WRITELN(' The given polynomials were not
                    linear.')
        else
            begin
                RESULT[A] := FIRST[B] * SECOND[B] ;
                RESULT[B] := FIRST[B] * SECOND[A] +
                            FIRST[A] * SECOND[B] ;
                RESULT[C] := FIRST[C] * SECOND[C]
            end
    end ;   (* of QUADMULTIPLY *)
```

Chapter 14 -- Selected Solutions

1.   Only A and D are invalid. If C or E tripped you up, recall that CHAR and BOOLEAN (and their subranges) are ordinal types.

2.   A, B, D, and F are true.

Chapter 15 -- Selected Solutions

1.   a)   INTEGER
     b)   REMINDER
     c)   (invalid)
     d)   DATE
     e)   STRING
     f)   CHAR
     g)   (invalid)
     h)   DATE

3.   f and g are not possible because the type of a set must be ordinal.

Chapter 16 -- <u>Selected Solutions</u>

1.  ```
    program TEXTCOUNT(INPUT,OUTPUT,TEXTFILE)  ;
    var
          TEXTFILE : TEXT  ;
          CHARCOUNT,LINECOUNT : INTEGER ;
    begin
          RESET(TEXTFILE) ;
          CHARCOUNT := 0  ;
          LINECOUNT := 0  ;
          while not EOF(TEXTFILE) do
            begin
                LINECOUNT := LINECOUNT + 1  ;
                while not EOLN(TEXTFILE) do
                    begin
                      GET(TEXTFILE)  ;
                      CHARCOUNT := CHARCOUNT + 1
                    end
            end  ;
          WRITELN(CHARCOUNT,' characters were
                        read.')  ;
          WRITELN(LINECOUNT,' lines were read,')
    end.
    ```

4. This loop skips over the characters in INPUT until a question mark is found.

5. All except <u>F</u> are possible.

Chapter 17 -- <u>Selected Solutions</u>

4.  ```
    function FINDNODE(BASE : TREELINK;
                      NODE : STRING) : BOOLEAN ;
    begin
          if BASE = nil then
            FINDNODE := FALSE
          else
            with BASE↑ do
              if DATA = NODE then
                FINDNODE := TRUE
              else
                FINDNODE := FINDNODE(LEFT,NODE)
                            or FINDNODE(RIGHT,
                                        NODE)
    end ;  (* of FINDNODE *)
    ```

```
6.    function EQUALTREE(BASE1,BASE2 : TREELINK)  :
         BOOLEAN ;
      begin
        EQUALTREE := FALSE ;
        if BASE1 = BASE2 then
           EQUALTREE := TRUE
        else
          if (BASE1 <> nil) and (BASE2 <> nil)
               then
               if BASE1↑.DATA = BASE2↑.DATA then
                  EQUALTREE   := EQUALTREE(BASE1↑.
                              LEFT,BASE2↑.LEFT)
                              and EQUALTREE(BASE1↑
                              .RIGHT,BASE2↑.RIGHT)
      end ;  (* of EQUALTREE *)

7.    procedure PRUNETREE(BASE : TREELINK) ;
      begin
          in BASE <>  nil then
              begin
                 PRUNETREE(BASE↑.LEFT) ;
                 PRUNETREE(BASE↑.RIGHT) ;
                 DISPOSE(BASE)
              end
      end ;  (* of PRUNETREE *)

9.    procedure POSTORDER(BASE : TREELINK) ;
      begin
          if BASE <> nil then
              begin
                 POSTORDER(BASE↑.LEFT) ;
                 POSTORDER(BASE↑.RIGHT) ;
                 WRITELN(BASE↑.DATA)
              end
      end ;  (* of POSTORDER *)
```

Index